THE ORIGIN OF CAPITALISM

THE ORIGIN OF CAPITALISM

A Longer View

◆

ELLEN MEIKSINS WOOD

VERSO
London • New York

This edition first published by Verso 2002
© Ellen Meiksins Wood 2002
First published as *The Origin of Capitalism*
© Monthly Review Press, 1999

3 5 7 9 10 8 6 4 2

Verso
UK: 6 Meard Street, London W1F 0EG
USA: 180 Varick Street, New York NY 10014-4606
www.versobooks.com

Verso is the imprint of New Left Books

ISBN 1–85984–680–7
ISBN 1–85984–392–1 (pbk)

British Library Cataloguing in Publication Data
A catalogue record for this book is available from the British Library

Library of Congress Cataloging-in-Publication Data
A catalog record for this book is available from the Library of Congress

Typeset in 10pt Bembo by SetSystems, Saffron Walden, Essex
Printed and bound in Great Britain by Biddles Ltd, www.biddles.co.uk

CONTENTS

ACKNOWLEDGEMENTS

In the first edition, I thanked Neal Wood for his comments and encouragement, and Chris Phelps, who, when he was Editorial Director of Monthly Review Press, talked me into producing the book and also gave me some extremely useful and insightful criticisms and suggestions, not just editorial but substantive. In this substantially revised and expanded edition, I want to add thanks to George Comninel and Robert Brenner for their safety checks (though any remaining mistakes are, of course, my own), and their helpful suggestions, not to mention years of discussion on the relevant issues. My thanks also to Martin Paddio at MRP for his cooperation, against the odds; and to Sebastian Budgen at Verso for his constructive criticisms (as well as his role – together with other editors of *Historical Materialism* – in giving me an opportunity to rehearse in its pages some of the ideas on which this book is based). I'm also grateful to Justin Dyer for his careful and intelligent copy-editing, and to Tim Clark for his efficient guidance of the book through production.

INTRODUCTION

The 'collapse of Communism' in the late 1980s and 1990s seemed to confirm what many people have long believed: that capitalism is the natural condition of humanity, that it conforms to the laws of nature and basic human inclinations, and that any deviation from those natural laws and inclinations can only come to grief.

There are, of course, many reasons today for questioning the capitalist triumphalism that followed in the wake of the collapse. While I was writing the introduction to the first edition of this book, the world was still reeling from the Asian crisis. Today, the financial pages of the daily press are nervously watching the signs of recession in the US and rediscovering the old capitalist cycles that they had been assuring us were a thing of the past. The period between these two episodes has been punctuated in various parts of the world by a series of dramatic demonstrations that proudly describe themselves as 'anti-capitalist'; and, while many participants seem inclined to dissociate the evils of 'globalization' or 'neoliberalism' from the essential and irreducible nature of capitalism itself, they are very clear about the conflict between the needs of people and the requirements of profit, as manifested in everything from the growing gap between rich and poor to increasing ecological destruction.

In the past, capitalism has always pulled out of its recurrent crises, but never without laying a foundation for new and even worse ones. Whatever means have been found to limit or correct the damage, as many millions of people have often suffered from the cure as from the disease.

The increasingly transparent weaknesses and contradictions in the capitalist system may eventually convince even some of its more uncritical supporters that an alternative needs to be found. But the conviction that there is and can be no alternative is very deeply rooted, especially in Western culture. That conviction is supported not only by the more blatant expressions of capitalist ideology but also by some of our most cherished and unquestioned beliefs about history – not just the history of capitalism but history in general. It is as if capitalism has always been the destination of historical movement and, more than that, the movement of history itself has from the beginning been driven by capitalist 'laws of motion'.

BEGGING THE QUESTION

Capitalism is a system in which goods and services, down to the most basic necessities of life, are produced for profitable exchange, where even human labour-power is a commodity for sale in the market, and where all economic actors are dependent on the market. This is true not only of workers, who must sell their labour-power for a wage, but also of capitalists, who depend on the market to buy their inputs, including labour-power, and to sell their output for profit. Capitalism differs from other social forms because producers depend on the market for access to the means of production (unlike, for instance, peasants, who remain in direct, non-market possession of land); while appropriators cannot rely on 'extra-economic' powers of appropriation by means of direct coercion – such as the military, political, and judicial powers that enable feudal lords to extract surplus labour from peasants – but must depend on the purely 'economic' mechanisms of the market. This distinct system of market dependence means that the requirements of competition and profit-maximization are the fundamental rules of life. Because of those rules, capitalism is a system uniquely driven to improve the productivity of labour by technical means. Above all, it is a system in which the bulk of society's work is done by propertyless labourers who are obliged to sell their labour-power in exchange for a wage in order to gain access to the means of life and of labour itself. In the process of supplying the needs and wants of society, workers are at the same time and inseparably creating profits for those who buy their labour-power. In fact, the production of goods and services is subordinate to the production of capital and capitalist profit. The basic objective of the capitalist system, in other words, is the production and self-expansion of capital.

This distinctive way of supplying the material needs of human beings, so very different from all preceding ways of organizing material life and social reproduction, has existed for a very short time, barely a fraction of humanity's existence on earth. Even those who most emphatically insist on the system's roots in human nature and its natural continuity with age-old human practices would not claim that it *really* existed before the early modern period, and then only in Western Europe. They may see bits of it in earlier periods, or detect its beginnings in the Middle Ages as a looming threat to a declining feudalism but still constrained by feudal restrictions, or they may say that it began with the expansion of trade or with voyages of discovery – with, say, Columbus's explorations at the end of the fifteenth century. Some might call these early forms 'proto-capitalism', but few would say that the capitalist system existed in earnest before the sixteenth or seventeenth century, and some would place it as late as the eighteenth, or perhaps even the nineteenth, when it matured into its industrial form.

Yet, paradoxically, historical accounts of how this system came into being have typically treated it as the natural realization of ever-present tendencies. Since historians first began explaining the emergence of capitalism, there has scarcely existed an explanation that did not begin by assuming the very thing that needed to be explained. Almost without exception, accounts of the origin of capitalism have been fundamentally circular: they have assumed the prior existence of capitalism in order to explain its coming into being. In order to explain capitalism's distinctive drive to maximize profit, they have presupposed the existence of a universal profit-maximizing rationality. In order to explain capitalism's drive to improve labour-productivity by technical means, they have also presupposed a continuous, almost natural, progress of technological improvement in the productivity of labour.

These question-begging explanations have their origins in classical political economy and Enlightenment conceptions of progress. Together, they give an account of historical development in which the emergence and growth to maturity of capitalism are already prefigured in the earliest manifestations of human rationality, in the technological advances that began when *Homo sapiens* first wielded a tool, and in the acts of exchange human beings have practised since time immemorial. History's journey to that final destination, to 'commercial society' or capitalism, has, to be sure, been long and arduous, and many obstacles have stood in its way. But its progress has nonetheless been natural and inevitable. Nothing more is required, then, to explain the 'rise of capitalism' than an account of how the many obstacles to its forward movement have been lifted – sometimes gradually, sometimes suddenly, with revolutionary violence.

In most accounts of capitalism and its origin, there really *is* no origin. Capitalism seems always to *be* there, somewhere; and it only needs to be released from its chains – for instance, from the fetters of feudalism – to be allowed to grow and mature. Typically, these fetters are political: the parasitic powers of lordship, or the restrictions of an autocratic state. Sometimes they are cultural or ideological: perhaps the wrong religion. These constraints confine the free movement of 'economic' actors, the free expression of economic rationality. The 'economic' in these formulations is identified with exchange or markets; and it is here that we can detect the assumption that the seeds of capitalism are contained in the most primitive acts of exchange, in any form of trade or market activity. That assumption is typically connected with the other presupposition: that history has been an almost natural process of technological development. One way or another, capitalism more or less naturally appears when and where expanding markets and technological development reach the right level, allowing sufficient wealth to be accumulated so that it can be profitably reinvested. Many Marxist explanations are fundamentally the same – with the addition of bourgeois revolutions to help break the fetters.

The effect of these explanations is to stress the *continuity* between non-capitalist and capitalist societies, and to deny or disguise the *specificity* of capitalism. Exchange has existed more or less forever, and it seems that the capitalist market is just more of the same. In this kind of argument, because capitalism's specific and unique need constantly to revolutionize the forces of production is just an extension and an acceleration of universal and transhistorical, almost *natural*, tendencies, industrialization is the inevitable outcome of humanity's most basic inclinations. So the lineage of capitalism passes naturally from the earliest Babylonian merchant through the medieval burgher to the early modern bourgeois and finally to the industrial capitalist.[1]

There is a similar logic in certain Marxist versions of this story, even though the narrative in more recent versions often shifts from the town to the countryside, and merchants are replaced by rural commodity producers, small or 'middling' farmers waiting for the opportunity to blossom into full-blown capitalists. In this kind of narrative, petty commodity production, released from the bonds of feudalism, grows more or less naturally into capitalism, and petty commodity producers, just given the chance, will take the capitalist road.

Central to these conventional accounts of history are certain assumptions, explicit or implicit, about human nature and about how human beings will behave, if only given the chance. They will, so the story goes, always avail themselves of the opportunity to maximize profit through acts of exchange, and in order to realize that natural inclination, they will always find ways of improving the organization and instruments of work in order to enhance the productivity of labour.

OPPORTUNITY OR IMPERATIVE?

In the classic model, then, capitalism is an opportunity to be taken, wherever and whenever possible. This notion of *opportunity* is absolutely critical to the conventional understanding of the capitalist system, present even in our everyday language. Consider common usage of the word that lies at the very heart of capitalism: the 'market'. Almost every definition of *market* in the dictionary connotes an *opportunity*: as a concrete locale or institution, a market is a place where opportunities exist to buy and sell; as an abstraction, a market is the possibility of sale. Goods 'find a market', and we say there is a market for a service or commodity when there is a demand for it, which means it can and will be sold. Markets are 'opened' to those who want to sell. The market represents 'conditions as regards, opportunity for, buying and selling' (*The Concise Oxford Dictionary*). The market implies *offering* and *choice*.

What, then, are market *forces*? Doesn't force imply coercion? In capitalist ideology the market implies not compulsion but freedom. At the same time, this freedom is guaranteed by certain mechanisms that ensure a 'rational economy', where supply meets demand, putting on offer commodities and services that people will freely choose. These mechanisms are the impersonal 'forces' of the market, and if they are in any way coercive, it is simply in the sense that they compel economic actors to act 'rationally' so as to maximize choice and opportunity. This implies that capitalism, the ultimate 'market society', is the optimal condition of opportunity and choice. More goods and services are on offer, more people are more free to sell and profit from them, and more people are more free to choose among and buy them.

So what is wrong with this conception? A socialist is likely to say that the major missing ingredient is the commodification of labour-power and class exploitation. So far so good. But what may not always be so clear, even in socialist accounts of the market, is that the distinctive and dominant characteristic of the capitalist market is not opportunity or choice but, on the contrary, compulsion. Material life and social reproduction in capitalism are universally mediated by the market, so that all individuals must in one way or another enter into market relations in order to gain access to the means of life. This unique system of market-dependence means that the dictates of the capitalist market – its imperatives of competition, accumulation, profit-maximization, and increasing labour-productivity – regulate not only all economic transactions but social relations in general. As relations among human beings are mediated by the process of commodity exchange, social relations among people appear as relations among things: the 'fetishism of commodities', in Marx's famous phrase.

Some readers are likely to object here that this is something every socialist, or at least every Marxist, knows. But, as we shall see in what follows, the specificities of capitalism, like the operation of the capitalist market as imperative rather than as opportunity, tend to get lost even in Marxist histories of capitalism. The capitalist market as a specific social form disappears when the transition from pre-capitalist to capitalist societies is presented as a more or less natural, if often thwarted, extension or maturation of already existing social forms, at best a quantitative rather than a qualitative transformation.

This book is about the origin of capitalism and about the controversies it has evoked, both historical and theoretical. Part I surveys the most important historical accounts and the debates surrounding them. It deals in particular with the most common model of capitalist development, the so-called 'commercialization model', in several of its variants, and also with some of the main challenges to it. Parts II and III sketch an alternative history that,

I hope, avoids some of the most common pit-falls of the standard question-begging explanations, building on the debates discussed in Part I and especially on those histories that have challenged the prevailing conventions. This new, revised and expanded edition contains, among other things, new sections and chapters in which arguments are developed that were only hinted at in the first edition, especially about non-capitalist commerce, the origin of capitalist imperialism, and the relation between capitalism and the nation state.

I have added a subtitle to the original title, which I hope will convey not only the simple fact that this new edition is substantially longer than the old one but also the fact that I am taking what might be called a 'long view' of capitalism and its consequences. My first intention is to challenge the naturalization of capitalism and to highlight the particular ways in which it represents a historically specific social form and a historic rupture with earlier forms. But the purpose of this exercise is both scholarly and political. The naturalization of capitalism, which denies its specificity and the long and painful historical processes that brought it into being, limits our understanding of the past. At the same time, it restricts our hopes and expectations for the future, for if capitalism is the natural culmination of history, then surmounting it is unimaginable. The question of the origin of capitalism may seem arcane, but it goes to the heart of assumptions deeply rooted in our culture, widespread and dangerous illusions about the so-called 'free' market and its benefits to humanity, its compatibility with democracy, social justice and ecological sustainability. Thinking about future alternatives to capitalism requires us to think about alternative conceptions of its past.

PART I

Histories of the Transition

I

THE COMMERCIALIZATION MODEL AND ITS LEGACY

The most common way of explaining the origin of capitalism is to presuppose that its development is the natural outcome of human practices almost as old as the species itself, which required only the removal of external obstacles that hindered its realization. This mode of explanation, or non-explanation, which has existed in many variants, constitutes what has been called the 'commercialization model' of economic development, and this model is arguably still the dominant one. This is so even among its harshest critics. It is not entirely absent from the demographic explanations that claim to have displaced it, or even from most Marxist accounts.

THE COMMERCIALIZATION MODEL

The traditional account – which appears in classical political economy, Enlightenment conceptions of progress, and many more modern histories – is as follows. With or without a natural inclination to 'truck, barter, and exchange' (in Adam Smith's famous formulation), rationally self-interested individuals have been engaging in acts of exchange since the dawn of history. These acts became increasingly specialized with an evolving division of labour, which was also accompanied by technical improvements in the instruments of production. Improvements in productivity, in many of these explanations, may in fact have been the primary purpose of the increasingly specialized division of labour, so that there tends to be a close connection between these accounts of commercial development and a kind of technological determinism. Capitalism, then, or 'commercial society', the highest stage of progress, represents a maturation of age-old commercial practices (together with technical advances) and their liberation from political and cultural constraints.

Far from recognizing that the market became capitalist when it became compulsory, these accounts suggest that capitalism emerged when the market was liberated from age-old constraints and when, for one reason or another, opportunities for trade expanded. In these accounts, capitalism represents not so much a qualitative break from earlier forms as a massive quantitative increase: an expansion of markets and the growing commercialization of economic life.

But only in the West, the story goes, were these constraints comprehensively and decisively lifted. In the ancient Mediterranean, commercial society was already fairly well established, but its further evolution was interrupted by an unnatural break – the hiatus of feudalism, and several dark centuries during which economic life was again fettered by irrationalism and the political parasitism of landlordly power.

The classical explanation of this interruption invokes barbarian invasions of the Roman Empire, but a later and very influential version of this model was elaborated by the Belgian historian Henri Pirenne. Pirenne situated the rupture of the Mediterranean commercial civilization rather later, in the Muslim invasion, which, he argued, suppressed the old commercial system by closing off the Mediterranean trade routes between East and West. A growing 'economy of exchange', led by a professional class of merchants, was replaced by an 'economy of consumption', the rentier economy of the feudal aristocracy.[1]

But eventually, according to both Pirenne and his predecessors, commerce revived with the growth of cities and the liberation of merchants. Here we come to one of the most common assumptions associated with the commercialization model: the association of capitalism with cities – indeed, the assumption that cities are from the beginning capitalism in embryo. In the early modern period, Pirenne argued, cities emerged with distinctive and unprecedented autonomy, cities devoted to trade and dominated by an autonomous burgher (or bourgeois) class, which was to free itself once and for all from the fetters of the old cultural constraints and political parasitism. This liberation of the urban economy, of commercial activity and mercantile rationality, accompanied by the inevitable improvements in techniques of production that evidently follow from the emancipation of trade, was apparently enough to account for the rise of modern capitalism.

All these explanations have in common certain assumptions about the continuity of trade and markets, from their earliest manifestations in exchange to their maturity in modern industrial capitalism. The age-old practice of commercial profit-taking in the form of 'buying cheap and selling dear' is not, in these accounts, fundamentally different from capitalist exchange and accumulation through the appropriation of surplus value.

The origin of capitalism or 'commercial society', then, does not in this model represent a major social transformation so much as a quantitative increment. Commerce becomes more widespread and encompasses ever more commodities. It also brings with it ever more wealth – and here, in classical political economy, we encounter the notion that commerce and the economic rationality that it engenders – the prudence and frugality of rational economic actors engaged in commercial transactions – encourages the accumulation of sufficient wealth to permit investment. This 'previous' or 'primitive' accumulation, when it reaches a critical mass, brings commercialization to fruition in a mature 'commercial society'. This notion, 'the so-called primitive accumulation', would, as we shall see, become the focal point of a major shift in explaining the origin of capitalism, when Marx subjected it to critical scrutiny in Volume I of *Capital*.

There also tends to be another common theme in these histories of capitalism: the bourgeois as agent of progress. We have become so used to the identification of *bourgeois* with *capitalist* that the presuppositions secreted in this conflation have become invisible to us. The burgher or bourgeois is, by definition, a town-dweller. Beyond that, specifically in its French form, the word was once conventionally used to mean nothing more than someone of non-noble status who, while he worked for a living, did not generally dirty his hands and used his mind more than his body in his work. That old usage tells us nothing about capitalism, and is likely to refer to a professional, an officeholder, or an intellectual no less than to a merchant. The convergence of 'capitalist' and 'bourgeois' was implanted in Western culture by means of conceptions of progress that joined British economic development with the French Revolution, in a composite picture of historical change. In the slippage from town-dweller to capitalist via the merchant that occurs in the later uses of 'bourgeois', we can follow the logic of the commercialization model: the ancient town-dweller gives way to the medieval burgher, who in turn develops seamlessly into the modern capitalist. As a famous historian has sardonically described this process, history is the perennial rise of the middle classes.

This is not to say that all historians who subscribe to such models have failed to acknowledge that capitalism represents a historic break or transformation of one kind or another. It is true that some have tended to find not just trade but a bit of capitalism itself almost everywhere, especially in Greek and Roman antiquity, always just waiting to be released from extraneous impediments. But even they have generally insisted on a major shift from the economic principles of feudalism to the new rationality of 'commercial society' or capitalism. People have often talked, for example, about the transition from a 'natural' economy to a money economy, or even from production for use to production for exchange. Yet if there is a major transformation in these historical accounts, it is not in the nature of trade and markets themselves. The change is rather in what happens to the forces and institutions – political, legal, cultural, and ideological, as well as technological – that have impeded the natural evolution of trade and the maturation of markets.

If anything, in these models it is *feudalism* that represents the real historic rupture, interrupting the natural development of commercial society. The resumption of commercial development, beginning in the interstices of feudalism and then breaking through its constraints, is treated as a major change in the history of Europe, but it appears as a resumption of a historical process that was temporarily – if drastically and for a rather long time – deflected. These assumptions tend to have another important corollary, namely that towns and trade were by nature antithetical to feudalism, so that their growth, however it came about, undermined the foundations of the feudal system.

But if feudalism had derailed the progress of commercial society, according to these explanations, the intrinsic logic of the market never significantly changed. From the beginning, it involved rationally self-interested individuals maximizing their utilities by selling goods for profit whenever the opportunity presented itself. More particularly, it involved an increasing division of labour and specialization, requiring ever more elaborate networks of trade, and, above all, ever-improving productive techniques to cut costs and enhance commercial profits. This logic could in various ways be thwarted. It could even be more or less completely submerged – so that, for example, feudal lords could suppress it, appropriating wealth not by engaging in profitable exchange or encouraging the improvement of productive techniques but rather by exploiting forced labour, squeezing surpluses out of peasants by means of superior power. But in principle, the logic of the market remained ever the same: always an opportunity to be taken whenever possible, always conducive to economic growth and the improvement of productive forces, always bound eventually to produce industrial capitalism, if left free to work out its natural logic.

In other words, the commercialization model made no acknowledgement of imperatives specific to capitalism, of the specific ways in which the market operates in capitalism, of its specific laws of motion that uniquely compel people to enter the market, to reinvest surpluses and to produce 'efficiently' by improving labour productivity – the laws of competition, profit-maximization, and capital accumulation. It follows that adherents of this model saw no need to explain the specific social property relations and the specific mode of exploitation that determine these specific laws of motion.

There was, in fact, no need in the commercialization model to explain the emergence of capitalism at all. It assumed that capitalism had existed, at least in embryo, from the dawn of history, if not in the very core of human nature and human rationality. People, it assumed, given the chance, have always behaved according to the rules of capitalist rationality, pursuing profit and in its pursuit seeking ways to improve labour-productivity. So history in effect had proceeded by the laws of capitalist development, in a process of economic growth sustained by developing productive forces, albeit with some major interruptions. If the emergence of a mature capitalist economy required any explanation, it was to identify the barriers that have stood in the way of its natural development, and the process by which those barriers were lifted.

There is, of course, a major paradox here. The market was supposed to be an arena of choice, and 'commercial society' the perfection of freedom. Yet this conception of the market seems to rule out human freedom. It has tended to be associated with a theory of history in which modern capitalism is the outcome of an almost natural and inevitable process, following certain universal, transhistorical, and immutable laws. The operation of these laws can, at least temporarily, be thwarted, but not without great cost. Its end product, the 'free' market, is an impersonal mechanism that can to some extent be controlled and regulated, but that cannot finally be thwarted without all the dangers – and the futility – entailed by any attempt to violate the laws of nature.

AFTER THE CLASSIC
COMMERCIALIZATION MODEL

There have been various refinements of the basic commercialization model, from Max Weber to Fernand Braudel.[2] Weber certainly did not fail to see that a fully developed capitalism emerged only in very specific historical conditions and not in others. He was more than willing to see some kind of capitalism in earlier times, even in classical antiquity. But he did, after all, set out to distinguish Europe from other parts of the world, and he did, of course, emphasize the uniqueness of the Western city and European religion, especially in order to explain the unique development of Western capitalism. The point, however, is that he always tended to talk about the factors that *impeded* the development of capitalism in other places – their kinship forms, their forms of domination, their religious traditions, and so on – as if the natural, *un*impeded growth of towns and trade and the liberation of towns and burgher classes would by definition mean capitalism. Weber also, it should be added, shares with many others the assumption that the development of capitalism was a trans-European (or Western European) process – not only that certain general European circumstances were necessary conditions for capitalism but that all of Europe, for all its internal variations, followed essentially one historical path.

More recently, there have been frontal attacks on the commercialization model in general and the Pirenne thesis in particular, which is now generally out of favour. Among the most recent and influential of these has been the demographic model, which attributes European economic development to certain autonomous cycles of population growth and decline. But however vehemently the old model has been challenged, it is not really clear that the fundamental presuppositions of the demographic explanation are as far removed from the commercialization model as its exponents claim.

The underlying premise of the demographic model is that the transition to capitalism was determined by the laws of supply and demand.[3] Those laws might be determined in more complicated ways than the commercialization model could account for. They might have less to do with the social processes of urbanization and growing trade than with complex cyclical patterns of population growth and decline, or Malthusian blockages. But the transition to capitalism is still a response to the universal and transhistorical laws of the market, the laws of supply and demand. The nature of the market and its laws is never really questioned.

The demographic model certainly challenges the primacy of expanding trade as a determinant in European economic development. It may not even deny, at least explicitly, that the capitalist market is qualitatively different from, and not just quantitatively larger and more inclusive than, markets in non-capitalist societies. But neither does it represent a frontal challenge to that convention, and in effect takes the convention for granted.

Another influential explanation has sometimes been associated with 'world systems' theory, especially where it intersects with 'dependency' theory, according to which economic development in a 'world' economy is largely determined by an unequal exchange between regions, between 'core' and 'periphery', and especially the exploitation of the colonial (and post-colonial) world by imperial powers.[4] According to some applications of this theory, capitalism originated in the context of such a 'world' economy, which emerged in the early modern period, if not before, when vast trading networks covered the globe. A central theme here is that even the most advanced civilizations of the non-European world, whose commercial and technological development far exceeded that of Europe on the eve of its breakthrough to a mature capitalism, were blocked by these imbalances. While their accumulation of wealth was impeded by uneven exchange and imperial exploitation, the European beneficiaries of these unequal relations accumulated disproportionately and were therefore able to make the final leap to capitalism, especially in its industrial form, by investing their accumulated wealth.

It has also been suggested by major advocates of the world systems theory that the West had certain other advantages. In particular, the fragmented state-form of feudalism and the nation states that followed it, while encouraging the development of a trade-based division of labour, did not act as a drag on commerce and accumulation. By contrast, the imperial states of the great non-European civilizations sapped commercial wealth and prevented its reinvestment.

This account has much in common with the old commercialization model. The extent of trade is the index of capitalist development, which arises from the growth of commercial activity and the 'primitive accumulation' that follows from it. Economies develop in a capitalist direction to the extent that the expansion of trade and the accumulation of commercial wealth is free from impediments. Just as the old model treated the emergence of 'commercial society' as a more or less natural process in the absence of obstacles, this world systems theory to a significant extent shares that view or simply inverts it: if some already well-developed economies *failed* to produce a mature capitalism, it was because they were thwarted by obstacles put in their way.

In yet another variation on the old commercialization theme, it has been suggested that capitalism was the result of an incremental process in which, as the centre of commercial gravity shifted from one European locale to another – from the Italian city-states to the Netherlands or the cities of the Hanse, and from Spanish colonial expansion to other imperialisms, culminating in the British Empire – each built upon the accomplishments of the last, not only expanding the reach of European trade but also refining its instruments, such as the techniques of double-entry book-keeping in Italy or various financial innovations and improvements in productive technologies, especially in the Netherlands, culminating in the English Industrial Revolution. The end result of this 'value-added process' (perhaps with the help of bourgeois revolutions) was modern capitalism.[5]

In one way or another, then, whether by processes of urbanization and growing trade or by the cyclical patterns of demographic growth, the transition to capitalism in all these explanations is a quantitative expansion of commercial activity and the universal and transhistorical laws of the market. Needless to say, neo-classical economics has done nothing to displace these assumptions – not least because it is generally uninterested in history altogether. As for historians today, those interested in the *longue durée* are likely to belong to the demographic school, unless they are more interested in *mentalité* or discourse than in economic processes. Others, especially in the English-speaking world, are generally suspicious of long-term processes altogether and are more interested in very local or episodic histories and in proximate causes. They do not actually *challenge* the existing theories of long-term development so much as they merely dismiss or evade them.[6]

The new wave of historical sociology is different. It is, of course, primarily interested in long-term processes of social change. But even here there is a tendency to beg the question in various ways. For instance, in one of the most important recent works in this genre, Michael Mann explicitly adopts what he calls a 'teleological bias', according to which industrial capitalism is already prefigured in medieval European social arrangements.[7] Not surprisingly, for all its complexities, his argument situates the driving force of European development in the 'acceleration of intensive powers of economic praxis' and the 'extensive growth of commodity circuits' – in other words, technological progress and commercial expansion.[8] This explanation depends, yet again, on the absence of constraints: capitalism was free to develop in Europe because an essentially 'acephalous' social organization (the decentralized, fragmented political order of feudalism) left various actors (notably merchants) a substantial degree of autonomy (with the help of the 'rationalism' and normative order provided by Christianity). Furthermore, private property was allowed to develop into *capitalist* property because no community or class organization possessed monopoly powers. In short, not only the emergence of capitalism but also its eventual and apparently inevitable maturation into its industrial form are explained above all by a series of absences. If only by default, then, the traditional 'commercialization model' still prevails, whether on the surface or in more subterranean form.

A NOTABLE EXCEPTION: KARL POLANYI

In his classic *The Great Transformation* (1944), and other works, the economic historian and anthropologist Karl Polanyi maintained that the motive of individual profit associated with market exchange was never till the modern age the dominant principle of economic life.[9] Even where markets were well developed, a sharp distinction must be made, he said, between societies with markets, such as have existed throughout recorded history, and a 'market society'. In all earlier societies, 'economic' relations and practices were 'embedded' or submerged in non-economic – kinship, communal, religious, and political – relationships. There have been other motives driving economic activity than the purely 'economic' motives of profit and material gain, such as the achievement of status and prestige, or the maintenance of communal solidarity. There have been other ways of organizing economic life than through the mechanisms of market exchange, in particular 'reciprocity' and 'redistribution' – elaborate reciprocal obligations determined, for instance, by kinship, or the authoritative appropriation of surpluses by some kind of central political or religious power and their redistribution from the centre.

Polanyi directly challenged Adam Smith's assumptions about

'economic man' and his natural 'propensity to truck, barter, and exchange', arguing that this 'propensity' had never before Smith's own time played the dominant role he assigned to it, and that it did not *regulate* the economy until a century later. Where markets did exist in pre-market societies, even where they were extensive and important, they remained a subordinate feature of economic life, dominated by other principles of economic behaviour. Not only that, these markets, even in the most wide-ranging and complex commercial systems, operated according to a logic quite distinct from that of the modern capitalist market.

In particular, neither the local markets nor the long-distance trade characteristic of pre-capitalist economies were essentially competitive (let alone, he might have added, *driven* by competition). These forms of trade – between town and country in the one case and climatic zones in the other – were, he suggests, more 'complementary' than competitive – even, evidently, when 'complementarity' was distorted by unequal power relations. External trade was simply 'carrying' trade. Here, the merchant's job was to move goods from one market to another, while in local trade, Polanyi argued, commercial activity was strictly regulated and exclusive. In general, competition was deliberately eliminated because it tended to disorganize trade.

Polanyi points out that only internal, national markets – a very late development, much resisted by local merchants and autonomous towns in the most advanced commercial centres of Europe – were to be conducted according to competitive principles. But even internal markets within early modern European nation states were for some time simply a loose collection of separate municipal markets, joined by a carrying trade hardly different in principle from long-distance, overseas commerce. Nor was an integrated internal market a direct descendant of, or a natural evolution from, the local or long-distance trade that preceded it. It was, Polanyi argues, a product of state intervention – and even then, in an economy still largely based on production by self-sufficient peasant households labouring for subsistence, state regulation continued to prevail over competitive principles.

Only in modern 'market society', according to Polanyi, is there a distinct 'economic' motive, distinct economic institutions and relations separated from non-economic relations. Because human beings and nature – in the form of labour and land – are treated, however fictitiously, as commodities in a self-regulating system of markets driven by the price mechanism, society itself becomes an 'adjunct' of the market. A market *economy* can exist only in 'market *society*', that is, a society where, instead of an economy embedded in social relations, social relations are embedded in the economy.

Polanyi was not, of course, alone in noting the secondary role of the market in pre-capitalist societies. Any competent economic historian or anthropologist is bound to acknowledge the various non-market principles of economic behaviour that operated in such societies, from the most 'primitive' and egalitarian to the most elaborate, stratified, and exploitative 'high' civilizations. Other economic historians (though perhaps not as many as one might imagine) have also taken note of certain changes in the principles of trade. But Polanyi's account is particularly notable for its stark delineation of the rupture between a market society and the non-market societies that preceded it, even societies with markets – not only the differences between their economic logics but also the social dislocations that that transformation brought about. So disruptive was the system of self-regulating markets, Polanyi insists, not only to social relations but also to the human psyche, so awful were its effects on human lives, that the history of its implantation had to be at the same time the history of protection from its ravages. Without 'protective countermoves', particularly by means of state intervention, 'human society would have been annihilated'.[10]

This argument in many ways represents a dramatic departure from accounts of economic development that stress the (more or less benign) continuities between ancient commerce and the modern capitalist economy, even when they observe the antagonism between 'commercial' or capitalist principles and the economic (or anti-economic) logic of feudalism. But in some important respects, Polanyi's account retains significant affinities with more conventional economic histories. The main problems have to do with his explanation of the conditions in which market society emerged, the historical process that brought it into being, and what this implies about his understanding of the market as a social form. This is not the place to enter into a detailed debate about the nature of medieval English land tenure, 'mercantilism', the Speenhamland system, or other specific historical questions about which specialists today would have reason to take issue with Polanyi. The issue here is the broader sweep of Polanyi's historical narrative and its consequences for our understanding of modern capitalism.

There is, first, more than a little technological determinism in his argument. The main theme of Polanyi's historical account is how the Industrial Revolution brought about a market society – how, in a commercial society, the invention of complex machines made it necessary to convert 'the natural and human substance of society into commodities'.[11] 'Since elaborate machines are expensive, they do not pay unless large amounts of goods are produced', he wrote, and to achieve the necessary scale of production, production must be uninterrupted, which means that, for the merchant, 'all factors involved must be on sale'.[12] The ultimate and most disastrous step in creating the necessary conditions – that is, in creating the market society originally required by complex machine production – is the transformation of labour into a commodified 'factor'.

The sequence of causation here is significant. The Industrial Revolution was 'merely the beginning' of an 'extreme and radical' revolution that utterly transformed society by commodifying humanity and nature.[13] That transformation, then, was the effect of technological progress. At its heart was 'an almost miraculous improvement in the tools of production';[14] and, while it brought about a transformation of society, it was itself the culmination of earlier improvements in productivity, both in techniques and in the organization of land use, notably enclosures in England.

Although Polanyi takes issue with the belief in 'spontaneous progress', he never for a moment seems to doubt the inevitability of such improvements, at least in the context of Western commercial society, with its 'free institutions', especially its free urban communes, and the expansion of trade – what he calls 'the Western European trend of economic progress'.[15] His argument against conventional views of spontaneous progress is simply that they fail to consider the role of the state in affecting – and, more particularly, retarding – the rate of change (as the Tudor and early Stuart state retarded enclosure). Without such interventions, 'the rate of that progress might have been ruinous, and have turned the process itself into a degenerative instead of a constructive event', just as the Industrial Revolution itself required state intervention to preserve the social fabric.[16]

The main outlines of Polanyi's historical narrative, then, are in some respects not entirely different from the old commercialization model: the expansion of markets goes hand in hand with technological progress to produce modern industrial capitalism. And although the process culminates in England, it is a general European process. For that matter, it appears that the process that led from commercialization to industrialization to 'market society' may after all have been a more or less natural development in an increasingly commercialized world, a development completed only in Europe simply because certain non-economic obstacles did not here block its path. As a student of Polanyi's has explained in an account of his lectures on 'General Economic History', Polanyi argued that, in contrast to an equally commercialized East, Western European feudalism was not characterized by strong bonds of kinship, clan, and tribe, so that 'when feudal ties weakened and disappeared, there was little to stand in the way of

domination by market forces'. And while government intervention was required to create factor markets, 'the developing market
economy helped to destroy feudal economic and political
institutions'.[17]

What fails to emerge from all of this is an appreciation of the
ways in which a radical transformation of social relations *preceded*
industrialization. The revolutionizing of productive forces *presupposed* a transformation of property relations and a change in the
form of exploitation that created a historically unique *need* to
improve the productivity of labour. It *presupposed* the emergence
of capitalist imperatives: competition, accumulation, and profit-
maximization. To say this is not just to accuse Polanyi of putting
the cart before the horse. The more fundamental point is that his
order of causation suggests a failure to treat the capitalist market
itself as a specific social form. The specific imperatives of the
capitalist market – the pressures of accumulation and increasing
labour-productivity – are treated not as the product of specific
social relations but as a result of technological improvements that
seem more or less inevitable, at least in Western Europe.

The fact remains that *The Great Transformation* was a significant
departure from conventional historiography on the 'transition'.
Yet it is striking how little that important book has managed to
affect the dominant model, even though there now seems to be a
revival of interest in Polanyi. In general, we are still where we
were. Either the question of capitalism and its origins does not
arise at all, or else, even when questions are raised about how and
why capitalism *did* emerge in some special case or cases, they tend
to be overtaken by another question: why did capitalism *not*
emerge in others? Some readers may, for example, be familiar
with the idea of 'failed transitions' as a way of describing what
happened – or failed to happen – in the commerical city-states of
northern Italy, or in the Netherlands. That phrase 'failed transition' says it all.

ANTI-EUROCENTRISM

The question-begging assumptions of the old commercialization model can appear in the most unlikely places. For example, critics who accuse historians, and often Western Marxists in particular, of being 'Eurocentric' may, paradoxically, be reproducing the very assumptions that make the commercialization model the most Eurocentric of all.

That model was based on the premise that Europe deserves the credit for lifting barriers to the natural development of capitalism, permitting it to grow to maturity from its origins in urban society and trade. At least some anti-Eurocentric arguments proceed by challenging European primacy in that achievement. But it is hard to see the advantage of arguing that non-European societies with more highly developed urban civilizations and trading systems were further down the road of capitalist develop-ment than is acknowledged by Eurocentric versions of the model. That seems a peculiarly ineffective challenge to the old model and its naturalization of capitalism, accepting that model's very first premise. More particularly, such arguments tend to reinforce the deeply Eurocentric view that the absence of capitalism is somehow a historic failure (a rather counterproductive line of thought for *critics* of capitalism).

There are, to begin with, serious problems involved in lump-ing together a very wide variety of writers in the category 'Euro-centrism', as if they were all centred on Europe in the same way, and as if they all shared the same contempt for non-Europeans.[18] The category includes racists who insist on the natural superiority of Europeans over Asians, Africans, and indigenous Americans; cultural chauvinists who think that, for whatever reason, 'the West' has achieved a higher level of cultural development and 'rationality' that has given it an advantage in every other respect; environmental determinists who believe that Europe has some distinct ecological advantages; non-racist historians who neglect or underestimate the role of Western imperialism in European history; and Marxists who are neither racists, nor cultural chauvinists, nor ecological determinists, nor inclined to underestimate the evils of imperialism, but who believe that certain specific historical conditions in Europe, which have nothing to do with European superiority, produced certain specific historical consequences – such as the rise of capitalism.

Still, no one can deny that there is such a thing as European 'cultural arrogance', and we do have to accept that there are more than enough reasons to challenge conceptions of history that place Europeans at the centre of the universe, to the detriment, or the exclusion, of everyone else. The idea of 'Eurocentrism', for all its faults, should at least put us on guard against such cultural practices. It is, then, particularly puzzling that anti-Eurocentric histories of capitalism are generally based on the most Eurocentric assumptions.

As we have seen, in the old commercialization model so deeply embedded in Western culture, capitalism is conceived as a more or less natural outcome of age-old and virtually universal human practices, the activities of exchange, which have taken place not only in towns since time immemorial but also in agricultural societies. In some versions of this commercialization model, these practices are even treated as the expression of a natural human inclination to 'truck, barter, and exchange'. In other words, in these accounts capitalism really has no beginning, and its development involves no real transition from one mode of production to a very different one. They tend to take capitalism for granted, to assume its latent existence from the dawn of history, and to 'explain' its development, at best, by describing how *obstacles* to its natural progression were removed in some places as distinct from others.

Of course, in these accounts 'the West' has been most successful in throwing off the various shackles that impede economic development. Europeans have, for instance, replaced 'parasitic' political and legal forms, like feudalism or certain kinds of monarchy, with new forms of political liberty, from constitutional monarchy to liberal democracy. They have replaced superstitions with 'rationalism' – which means everything from Enlightenment philosophy to scientific and technological advances and economic 'rationality'. Above all, they have liberated the agents of progress, merchants or 'bourgeois', the bearers of reason and freedom, who only needed to throw off their feudal chains so that they could move history forward along its natural and preordained path.

How, then, do anti-Eurocentric histories differ from these classic explanations of the origin of capitalism? Anti-European critiques generally take one or both of two forms: first, they deny the 'superiority' of Europe and emphasize the importance, in fact the dominance, of non-European economies and trading networks throughout most of human history, as well as the level of technological development achieved by some of the main actors; and/or, second, they emphasize the importance of European imperialism in the development of capitalism. Often this has to do with the role of British imperialism, particularly the profits of sugar plantations and the slave trade, in the development of *industrial* capitalism, though 1492 is also a major milestone in the earlier rise of capitalism. These two theses may be combined in the argument that the dominant non-European trading powers did produce capitalism, though further development was thwarted, or at least that they could and probably would have produced it, if only Western imperialism had not robbed them of their wealth.

Now clearly, no serious historian today would deny the importance of trade and technology in Asia and other parts of the non-European world, or, for that matter, the relatively modest level of development attained by Europeans before the rise of capitalism. Nor would any such historian, especially on the left, deny the importance of imperialism in European history and the tremendous damage it has done. But the question is what this has to do with capitalism, and on that score, the anti-Eurocentric arguments tend to fall into precisely those Eurocentric traps they are meant to avoid.

The remarkable thing about anti-Eurocentric critiques is that they start from the same premises as do the standard Eurocentric explanations, the same commercialization model and the same conception of primitive accumulation. Traders or merchants anywhere and everywhere are potential, if not actual, capitalists, and the more active, wide-ranging, and wealthy they are, the further they are along the road of capitalist development. In that sense, many parts of Asia, Africa, and the Americas were well on their way to capitalism before European imperialism, in one way or another, blocked their path.

None of these critics seems to deny that, at some point, Europe did diverge from other parts of the world, but this divergence is associated with 'bourgeois revolution' and/or with the advent of industrial capitalism, once enough wealth had been accumulated by means of trade and imperial expropriation. Since trade was widespread in other parts of the world, imperialism was the really essential factor in distinguishing Europe from the rest, because it gave European powers the critical mass of wealth that finally differentiated them from other commercial powers.

These accounts tend to suggest not only that European development was basically the rise to power of the bourgeoisie, but also that advanced and wealthy non-European civilizations are, in effect, cases of arrested development because, even if through no fault of their own, they never did throw off their shackles by means of bourgeois revolution. And here, too, just as in classical political economy and its notion of 'primitive accumulation', the leap forward to 'modern' capitalism occurred because the bourgeoisie had managed, in one way or another, to accumulate sufficient wealth.

In the classic conception, as we have seen, 'primitive accumulation' is the prior accumulation of 'capital', which is here indistinguishable from any other kind of wealth or profit, and capitalism is basically more of the same, allowing reinvestment. 'Primitive accumulation' is 'primitive' only in the sense that it represents the accumulation of the mass of wealth required before 'commercial society' can reach maturity. In that sense, it is very much like the anti-Eurocentric conception of early 'capital accumulation', which reached the critical mass that made possible a 'mature' capitalism (or, in the terms of classical political economy, 'commercial society'). Like classical political economy, such anti-Eurocentric arguments evade the issue of the *transition* to capitalism by presupposing its existence in earlier forms.

As we shall see in the next chapter, a decisive break from the classic model came with Marx's critique of political economy and its notion of 'primitive accumulation', his definition of capital not simply as wealth or profit but also as a social relation, and his emphasis on the transformation of social property relations as the *real* 'primitive accumulation'. Yet critics of Eurocentric history have more or less returned to the old notion. Even at the point where they diverge most emphatically from the classic Eurocentric histories, in their emphasis on European imperialism as the chief impediment to non-European development, they simply invert an old Eurocentric principle: in the old accounts, Europe surpassed all other civilizations by removing obstacles to the natural development of 'commercial society'; in the anti-Eurocentric inversion, the failure of non-Europeans to complete the process of development, despite the fact that they had already come so far, was caused by obstacles created by Western imperialism.

So here again there seems to be no conception of capitalism as a specific social form, with a distinctive social structure and distinctive social relations of production, which compel economic agents to behave in specific ways and generate specific laws of motion. Here again there is no real transition. In much the same way that the old Eurocentric arguments took capitalism for granted, this one too avoids explaining the origin of this specific social form − or, to be more precise, denies its specificity and hence evades the question of its origin − by assuming its prior existence (sometimes called 'proto-capitalism', not to mention even earlier forms of trade and mercantile activity). There is no explanation of how a new social form came into being. Instead, the history of capitalism is a story in which age-old social practices, with no historical beginning, have grown and matured – unless their growth and maturation have been thwarted by internal or external obstacles.

There are, of course, variations on the old themes, most of all the attack on imperialism. There are also other refinements like the idea of 'bourgeois revolution' – though even this idea, no matter how much it is dressed up in Marxist trappings, is not fundamentally different from Eurocentric-bourgeois accounts that treat the bourgeoisie as agents of progress and credit them with throwing off the feudal shackles that impeded it. But whatever variations are introduced into the story, basically capitalism is just a lot more of what already existed in proto-capitalism and long before: more money, more urbanization, more trade, and more wealth.

Such anti-Eurocentric arguments suggest that an emphasis on the historical specificity of capitalism, its distinctive nature and its specific historical origin, is a brand of Eurocentrism. Yet surely there is no more effective way to puncture the Western sense of superiority than to challenge the triumphalist conviction that the Western path of historical development is the natural and inevitable way of things. It seems completely self-defeating to try to challenge this triumphalism by appropriating its most basic assumptions about the nature of capitalism. It is surely even more perverse to validate the superiority of capitalism by treating it as the universal standard of merit and progress. It is as if, by claiming capitalism for itself, Europe is appropriating all that is good and progressive, as if a different historical path represents failure, and as if we can affirm the value of other societies only by claiming that they really did develop capitalism (or at least proto-capitalism), or that they could and would have done so had history been allowed to take its natural course.

This is not to deny that much remains to be said about the connection between capitalism and imperialism. But to understand that connection – and to mount an effective challenge to Eurocentric neglect of Western imperialism – requires us to take into account the very specific conditions in which traditional forms of colonialism were transformed into capitalist types of imperialism. That means acknowledging the very specific effects of capitalist social property relations. This question will be taken up in Chapter 6.

2

MARXIST DEBATES

How we understand the history of capitalism has a great effect on how we understand the thing itself. The old models of capitalist development were a paradoxical blend of transhistorical determinism and 'free' market voluntarism, in which the capitalist market was both an immutable natural law and the perfection of human choice and freedom. The antithesis of such models would be a conception of the capitalist market that fully acknowledges its imperatives and compulsions, while recognizing that these imperatives are rooted not in some transhistorical natural law but in historically specific social relations, constituted by human agency and subject to change. This is the kind of conception we might expect to find in Marxism, but Marxist historians have not consistently provided that kind of alternative.

In historical debates about the origin of capitalism, there has been as much disagreement among Marxists as between Marxist and non-Marxist historians. Many Marxists have been no less wedded than anyone else to the old commercialization model, often, perhaps, with an even stronger dose of technological determinism. Others have been very critical of that model, though even here some residues remain. With the debate still in progress, there is still much work to be done.

Marx on the Transition

Matters are not helped by the fact that there are two different narratives in Marx's own work.[1] One is very much like the conventional model, where history is a succession of stages in the division of labour, with a transhistorical process of technological progress, and the leading role assigned to burgher classes who seem to bring about capitalism just by being liberated from feudal chains. In fact, capitalism already exists in feudalism, in a way, in its 'interstices,' to use Marx's word, and it enters the mainstream of history when it 'bursts asunder' the fetters of the feudal system. This is in essence the narrative of such earlier writings as *The German Ideology* and *The Communist Manifesto*. There, the origin of capitalism is not so much explained as presupposed, as a new social form waiting to be released by the rising bourgeoisie when it finally throws off its feudal shackles. This is the narrative at least implicit in traditional Marxist ideas of 'bourgeois revolution'.

For Marx's truly distinctive 'Marxist' approach, we have to look to his critique of political economy, in the *Grundrisse* and *Capital*. Although that approach was obviously much more developed in his revolutionary analysis of contemporary capitalism, he did apply his critique to the historical question of the system's origin in his dissection of 'the so-called primitive accumulation' in Volume I of *Capital*. Here he decisively broke with the old paradigm and laid a foundation for important elaborations by later Marxist historians.

As we have seen, the classic commercialization model, first laid out systematically by Adam Smith, suggests that the prelude to 'commercial society' was a process of prior accumulation in which wealth was amassed by means of commercial acumen and frugality, eventually reaching a point at which it was sufficient to permit substantial investment. This process represents the 'primitive' accumulation of 'capital' – which simply means the collection of material wealth. Variations on this theme have continued to appear even in contemporary explanations of capitalist development, for instance in those accounts that explain the origin of capitalism as a result of 'capital' accumulation by means of colonial exploitation and unequal exchange. In these arguments, again, capitalism, or 'commercial society', is a quantitative expansion of commerce and wealth, and there is little conception of a *transition*, a qualitative shift, from one social system with its own 'laws of motion', to a very different one with a very different dynamic and very different conditions of existence.

Marx, in his critique of 'the so-called primitive accumulation', diverged sharply from classical political economy and its commercialization model. The general principles spelled out in his critique of political economy – in particular, his insistence that wealth by itself is not 'capital', and that capital was a specific social relation – are here applied to the transition from feudalism to capitalism. It follows from these principles that the mere accumulation of wealth was not the decisive factor in the origin of capitalism. The 'primitive accumulation' of classical political economy is 'so-called' because capital, as Marx defines it, is a social relation and not just any kind of wealth or profit, and accumulation as such is not what brings about capitalism. While the accumulation of wealth was obviously a necessary condition of capitalism, it was far from being sufficient or decisive. What transformed wealth into *capital* was a transformation of social property relations.

The essence of Marx's critique of 'the so-called primitive accumulation' (and people too often miss the significance of the phrase 'so-called') is that no amount of accumulation, whether from outright theft, from imperialism, from commercial profit, or even from the exploitation of labour for commercial profit, by itself constitutes capital, nor will it produce capitalism. The specific precondition of capitalism is a transformation of social property relations that generates capitalist 'laws of motion': the *imperatives* of competition and profit-maximization, a *compulsion* to reinvest surpluses, and a systematic and relentless *need* to improve labour-productivity and develop the forces of production.

The critical transformation of social property relations, in Marx's account, took place in the English countryside, with the expropriation of direct producers. In the new agrarian relations, landlords increasingly derived rents from the commercial profits of capitalist tenants, while many small producers were dispossessed and became wage labourers. Marx regards this rural transformation as the *real* 'primitive accumulation' not because it created a critical mass of wealth but because these social property relations generated new economic imperatives, especially the compulsions of competition, a systematic need to develop the productive forces, leading to new laws of motion such as the world had never seen before.

At the heart of this argument was Marx's insistence on the historical specificity of capitalism. This meant that capitalism had a historical beginning, in very specific historical conditions, and therefore it had a conceivable end. Capitalism was not the product of some inevitable natural process, nor was it the end of history.

THE TRANSITION DEBATE

The most important Marxist histories since Marx have built upon the foundations laid in his critique of primitive accumulation. We can leave out of account altogether the crudest kinds of technological determinism that have all too often passed as Marxist theories of history, concentrating instead on the most serious and challenging Marxist accounts.

In 1950, an exchange took place between the economist Paul Sweezy and the economic historian Maurice Dobb, whose *Studies in the Development of Capitalism* (1946) Sweezy had criticized. Their exchange expanded into a major debate among a wide range of distinguished, mainly Marxist, historians in the journal

Science & Society, which was later collected and published as a book.[2] What came to be known as the 'transition debate', has been a central reference point for discussion of the subject among Marxists – and others – ever since.

Dobb's work represented a major advance in understanding the transition. Like other work in this tradition, most notably the writings of the historian of medieval Europe, R. H. Hilton, his analysis undermined the foundations of the old model, calling into question some of its basic premises, especially the assumption that capitalism was simply a quantitative expansion of commerce and that the antithesis to feudalism, which dissolved it and gave rise to capitalism, was to be found in towns and in trade.

The central question at issue between Sweezy and Dobb was where to locate the 'prime mover' in the transition from feudalism to capitalism. Was the primary cause of the transition to be found within the basic, constitutive relations of feudalism, the relations between lords and peasants? Or was it external to those relations, located particularly in the expansion of trade?

Dobb and, in the ensuing debate, Hilton made profoundly important arguments demonstrating that trade was not in itself the solvent of feudalism. In fact, trade and towns were not inherently inimical to feudalism at all. Instead, feudalism was dissolved and capitalism brought about by factors internal to the primary relations of feudalism itself, in the class struggles between lords and peasants. Hilton in particular pointed out that Pirenne's argument had been shown to be empirically flawed, and he spelled out the ways in which money, trade, towns, and even the so-called 'commercial revolution' were not alien but, on the contrary, integral to the feudal system. This meant that, while there was undoubtedly a complex process in which these factors contributed to the transition, they could not be regarded as the solvent of feudalism.

Both Dobb and Hilton in various ways suggested that the dissolution of feudalism and the rise of capitalism resulted from the *liberation* of petty commodity production, its release from the fetters of feudalism, largely by means of class struggle between lords and peasants. Dobb, for example, argued that, while class struggle did not 'in any simple and direct way' give rise to capitalism, it did serve to

> modify the dependence of the petty mode of production upon feudal overlordship and eventually to shake loose the small producer from feudal exploitation. It is then from the petty mode of production (in the degree to which it secures independence of action, and social differentiation in turn develops within it) that capitalism is born.[3]

Similarly, Hilton, whose studies on medieval peasants and their struggles represent some of the most important work in the historiography of any period, traced the transition to struggles between lords and peasants. The pressures imposed by lords on peasants to transfer surplus labour was, he suggested, the root cause of improved production techniques and the basis for the growth of simple commodity production. At the same time, peasant resistance to those pressures was crucially important to the process of transition to capitalism, 'the freeing of peasant and artisan economies for the development of commodity production and eventually the emergence of the capitalist entrepreneur'.[4]

Sweezy, in his counter-argument, insisted that feudalism, for all its inefficiencies and instabilities, was intrinsically tenacious and resistant to change, and that the main moving force in its dissolution had to come from outside. The feudal system could tolerate, and indeed required, a certain amount of trade; but with the establishment of localized urban trading and trans-shipment centres based on long-distance trade (about which Sweezy cited the authority of Henri Pirenne), a process was set in train that encouraged the growth of production for exchange, in tension with the feudal principle of production for use.

Nevertheless, capitalism was not, Sweezy argued, the immediate outcome of this process. The expansion of trade was sufficient to dissolve feudalism, and to usher in a transitional phase of 'pre-capitalist commodity production' that was itself unstable, preparing the ground for capitalism in the seventeenth and eighteenth centuries; but there was a subsequent distinct phase in the development of capitalism. Sweezy here made the important point that '[w]e usually think of a transition from one social system to another as a process in which the two systems directly confront each other and fight it out for supremacy', but it would be a 'serious error' to think of the transition from feudalism to capitalism in these terms.[5]

Sweezy did not propose to explain the second phase of the process, but he raised some critical questions about explanations offered by others. Two in particular stand out. First, he expressed scepticism about the plausibility of the view – following from the conventional interpretation of Marx's theory of the 'really revolutionary way' to industrial capitalism – that industrial capitalists rose from the ranks of petty producers. He proposed instead that we should understand the 'really revolutionary way' as a process in which the producer, instead of growing from petty producer into merchant and capitalist, '*starts out* as both a merchant and an employer of wage-labour', and capitalist enterprises are launched fully fledged instead of in a gradual process emerging out of the putting-out system.[6]

Sweezy's second point was that the generalization of commodity production could not account for the rise of capitalism, and that highly developed commodity production – as, for instance, in medieval Italy or Flanders – did not necessarily produce capitalism.[7] In the course of his argument, he made another suggestive point. In opposition to Maurice Dobb's theory that the decline of feudalism resulted from the over-exploitation of peasants and the class conflicts engendered by it, Sweezy proposed that it might be 'more accurate to say that the decline of western European feudalism was due to the inability of the ruling class to maintain control over, and hence to exploit, society's labour power'.[8]

This summary is, of course, a gross abbreviation and simplification of the complex arguments offered by the participants in the debate, but it should be enough to raise some critical questions about the assumptions on which each side was operating. At first glance, the issue seems pretty clear: Dobb was attacking the commercialization model, while Sweezy was defending it. In fact, some time later the Marxist historian Robert Brenner accused Sweezy, together with others such as André Gunder Frank and Immanuel Wallerstein, of being 'neo-Smithian' precisely because of their adherence to something like the classic commercialization model as outlined first by Adam Smith.[9] Brenner made a powerful argument about the way some Marxists have effectively swallowed the assumptions of the old model, the tendency to treat the specific dynamic of capitalism – and its need for increasing labour-productivity – as an inevitable outcome of commercial expansion.

On the face of it, Sweezy's argument is, in its main outlines, completely consistent with the commercialization model, while Dobb's account is a frontal attack on it. Sweezy seems to proceed from the Pirenne thesis in particular, and more generally suggests a fundamental antagonism between the growing system of long-distance trade and the basic principles of feudalism, and sometimes ascribes to pre-capitalist economic actors a rationality specific to capitalism. By contrast, Dobb and Hilton insist that towns and trade were not by nature necessarily inimical to feudalism, that the 'prime mover' is to be found within the primary property relations of feudalism, and that class struggle between lords and peasants was central to the process.

Yet there is more to the debate than this. Dobb and Hilton certainly depart from the commercialization model by situating the 'prime mover' in the countryside instead of in the town, and by focusing on class struggle between appropriators and producers instead of on the expansion of trade. But one critical assumption stays the same: capitalism emerges when the fetters of feudalism are removed. Capitalism is somehow already present in the interstices of feudalism, just waiting there to be released.

Dobb and Hilton thus do not seem to be challenging all the basic assumptions of the commercialization model, and some of the questions raised by Sweezy go to the heart of the problems they leave unresolved. One point stands out in the arguments of Dobb and Hilton: the transition to capitalism is a matter of liberating or 'shaking loose' an economic logic already present in simple commodity production. We are left with the overwhelming impression that, given the chance, the commodity-producing peasant (and artisan) will grow into a capitalist. The centre of gravity in this argument has shifted away from the city to the countryside, and class struggle has been given a new role, but how different are the assumptions underlying this argument from some of the main premises of the commercialization model? How far are we from the premise that the capitalist market is an opportunity rather than an imperative, and that what requires explanation in accounting for the rise of capitalism is the removal of obstacles, the breaking of fetters, and not the creation of a wholly new economic logic? To be sure, class struggle is central to the process, but it serves above all as a means of removing obstacles to something that was already immanent.

The commercialization model and other related explanations effectively assume the existence of capitalism, or a capitalist rationality, in order to explain its emergence. Feudalism is confronted by an already existing capitalism, or at least an already existing capitalist logic of process, whose coming into being is never explained. The explanations offered by Marxists like Hilton and Dobb, while in many ways devastating to the commercialization model and to its assumptions about the antithesis of feudalism and commerce, have not entirely escaped this trap, because they still in some important respects assume the very thing that needs to be explained.

Nor do they offer an entirely convincing response to the question raised by Sweezy about the 'failure' of advanced commercial centres such as those of Italy and Flanders. Here again there is a tendency to take capitalism for granted by simply explaining the *obstacles* that prevented these commercial cities from reaching maturity. The question posed about Flanders or Italy is not so much why and in what circumstances did capitalist imperatives impose themselves on economic actors, as they did in England, but rather why and in what ways were economic actors in the 'failed' transitions unwilling or unable – not least for ideological or cultural reasons – to break away from their attachment to feudalism in order to create a new social form?[10]

As for Sweezy's doubts about the 'really revolutionary way', later in the debate he did withdraw some of his objections to the conventional interpretation of what Marx had in mind but not necessarily his objections to the idea itself. While he never fully explained the reasons for his unease about the idea that capitalism emerged as petty commodity producers transformed themselves into capitalists, he seemed to find it inherently implausible.

Whatever Sweezy's reservations may have been, there were indeed good grounds for his scepticism. From our vantage point here, the problem is not that the 'really revolutionary way' gives rising yeomen credit for creating capitalism. The problem is rather that they tend to be depicted as more or less freely choosing the capitalist road, once released from feudal impediments, while capitalism is treated as a more or less organic growth out of petty commodity production – even if bourgeois revolutions may be required to remove the final obstacles. Whatever Sweezy may have had in mind in his objection to the 'really revolutionary way', it would certainly be reasonable to say that something more is required to account for the disposition of producers to behave like capitalists than simply their liberation from restraints or their growth from 'middling' to large proprietors. In other words, there is a qualitative, not simply a quantitative, difference between petty commodity production and capitalism, a difference that remains to be explained.

PERRY ANDERSON ON ABSOLUTISM AND CAPITALISM

In the 1970s another influential Marxist, Perry Anderson, editor of *New Left Review*, published two magisterial volumes of what was intended to be a trilogy, beginning with a study of the transition from Graeco-Roman antiquity to European feudalism (*Passages from Antiquity to Feudalism*), continuing with an analysis of European absolutism (*Lineages of the Absolutist State*), and culminating in a study of bourgeois revolutions and the development of capitalism. Although that third volume, which was to complete his account of the transition to capitalism, has not yet appeared, there is much to be learned from the first two, especially *Lineages*, and from various bits and pieces elsewhere.

For our purposes, we can begin with Anderson's definition of feudalism as a mode of production defined by 'an organic *unity* of economy and polity', which took the form of a 'chain of parcellized sovereignties', together with a hierarchical chain of conditional property. State power was fragmented among feudal lords, and lordship represented a unity of political and economic power. The fragment of the state that feudal lords possessed – their political, juridical, and military powers – at one and the same time constituted their economic power to appropriate surplus labour from dependent peasants. Lordship was accompanied by 'a mechanism of surplus extraction', serfdom, in which 'economic exploitation and politico-legal coercion were fused'.[11]

But something happened that made this feudal formation unstable. The old feudal bonds were weakened by the commutation of feudal dues into money rents, and, more particularly, by the growth of a commodity economy. 'With the generalized commutation of dues into money rents,' Anderson argues, 'the cellular unity of political and economic oppression of the peasantry was gravely weakened, and threatened to become dissociated. The result was a *displacement* of politico-legal coercion upwards towards a centralized, militarized summit – the Absolutist State.'[12] In other words, in order to strengthen their weakened hold on the peasantry, feudal lords concentrated their formerly fragmented or parcellized coercive powers in a new kind of centralized monarchy.

Meanwhile, in the interstices of the fragmented feudal system, in the town, an economic sphere had emerged that was not controlled by the aristocracy. At the same time, these towns became the sites of technical innovations. Anderson concludes that, while 'the political order remained feudal . . . society became more and more bourgeois'.[13]

The emergence of absolutism represents a critical step in Anderson's argument about the rise of capitalism. Absolutism itself was not a capitalist or proto-capitalist state. It was, if anything, essentially feudal in its basic structure, 'a *redeployed and recharged apparatus of feudal domination*, designed to clamp the peasant masses back into their traditional social position'.[14] But it was a pivotal moment in the development of capitalism.

Ironically, the effect of this displacement upwards of feudal coercive power – at least its principal contribution to the evolution of capitalism, according to Anderson – was to *fracture* the unity of economy and polity that had characterized feudalism. On the one hand, political power was concentrated in the royal state. On the other hand, the economy began to achieve a certain autonomy. As politico-legal coercion was 'displaced upwards', the commodity economy and the 'bourgeois society' that had grown in the interstices of feudalism were liberated and allowed to develop on their own terms.

That, then, is Anderson's conception of absolutism in broad outline. And much of it is very illuminating, too. His characterization of the absolutist state as essentially feudal is especially useful, though it demands closer scrutiny. Keep in mind what Anderson means. The absolutist state was essentially feudal, he insists, because it represented the displacement upward and the centralization of the feudal lords' politico-legal coercive powers, separating those powers from economic exploitation. To put it another way, the absolutist state separated the two moments of exploitation: the process of surplus extraction, on the one hand, and the coercive power that sustains it, on the other. The two then continued in separate spheres. The feudal fusion of economy and polity started giving way to the separation characteristic of capitalism, leaving the 'economy' to evolve according to its own internal logic.

Now, there is another way of looking at absolutism, which is that it represents a centralization of feudal power in a different sense: namely that the monarchical state itself becomes a form of property, an instrument of appropriation, in ways analogous to feudal lordship. Economic and political power are still fused, but the lord appropriates rents while the state and its officeholders appropriate peasant surpluses in the form of tax.

Sometimes Anderson does seem to think of absolutism in these terms, as still a unity of economic and political spheres. But his whole argument that absolutism plays a pivotal role in the transition to capitalism depends on the essential function of the absolutist state in *separating* political and economic spheres. He is at great pains to emphasize that what gets 'centralized upwards' in the absolutist state is not the feudal *fusion* of political and economic spheres but rather the politico-legal or coercive moment of feudalism as distinct from the moment of economic exploitation. The absolutist state simply represents for him the politico-legal coercive power that enforces the economic exploitation that takes place on a different plane.

In effect, the displacement upward of feudal political power plays the same role in Anderson's argument as the removal of fetters does in other versions of the old model. In fact, it seems that absolutism is one, if not the, essential means by which the fetters of feudalism were removed from the economy. Absolutism, then, seems to have been a necessary transitional point between feudalism and capitalism. In any case, freed from direct political bondage, commodity production was able to grow, and the 'economy' could follow its own inclinations. Capitalism was the result of liberating the economy, removing the dead hand of feudalism, and unleashing the natural bearers of economic rationality, the burghers or bourgeois – although the process could not, apparently, be properly completed unless and until the bourgeoisie seized political power, by means of bourgeois revolutions, and transformed the state to its own specific needs.

There are certain serious empirical problems in this treatment of absolutism as an apparently essential phase in the transition from feudalism to capitalism. Not the least of these problems is the fact that English capitalism did not enjoy the benefit of absolutism, while French absolutism did not give rise to capitalism (about which more in Part II). If that is so, then it may be more plausible to argue that absolutism was not a transitional phase between feudalism and capitalism, but was, on the contrary, an alternative route out of feudalism. At any rate, it should at least be clear that in many fundamental ways, Anderson's account, like earlier explanations of the transition to capitalism, relies above all on the removal of fetters from a social form that already existed – more or less unexplained – within the interstices of feudalism.

For all the sophisticated complexity of Anderson's argument, it is a refinement – fascinating and in many ways illuminating, but no less a refinement – of the commercialization model. Echoes of that old explanation are even more audible in Anderson's most recent statement of his argument, in a review of Robert Brenner's book *Merchants and Revolution*. Anderson is commenting here on Brenner's account of capitalism as, in the first instance, a specifically English phemonenon:

> The idea of capitalism in one country, taken literally, is only a bit more plausible than that of socialism. For Marx the different moments of the modern biography of capital were distributed in cumulative sequence, from the Italian cities to the towns of Flanders and Holland, to the empires of Portugal or Spain and the ports of France, before being 'systematically combined in England at the end of the 17th century'. Historically, it makes better sense

to view the emergence of capitalism as a value-added process gaining in complexity as it moved along a chain of inter-related sites. In this story, the role of cities was always central. English landowners could never have started their conversion to commercial agriculture without the market for wool in Flemish towns – just as Dutch farming was by Stuart times in advance of English, not least because it was conjoined to a richer urban society.[15]

We should first take note that Marx, in the passage cited by Anderson, is explaining the 'genesis of the *industrial* capitalist', not the origins of *capitalism*, not the emergence of specifically capitalist 'laws of motion', nor specifically capitalist social relations, a specifically capitalist form of exploitation, or the imperatives of self-sustaining economic development.[16] Marx is trying to explain how the accumulation of wealth was converted in the right conditions – that is, in already capitalist social conditions (in England) – from simply the unproductive profits of usury and commerce into industrial capital. As for the origins of the capitalist *system*, the 'so-called primitive accumulation' – in Marx's terms, the expropriation of direct producers, in particular peasants – that gave rise to specifically capitalist social property relations and the dynamic associated with them, Marx situates it firmly in England and in the countryside.

Here too the conditions emerged for the unprecedented kind of *internal* market that Marx regarded as the *sine qua non* of industrial capitalism. Like Brenner after him, Marx acknowledges the need to explain the distinctiveness of England's development. Not the least of England's specificities, as Brenner points out, is that while other centres of production, even in the medieval period, had experienced export booms, early modern England was unique in maintaining industrial growth even in the context of declining overseas markets; in other words, albeit within a network of international trade, capitalism *indeed* in one country.[17]

But there is no need to get distracted here by speculations about Marx's views on the relation between agrarian and industrial capitalism (or about the questions he left unanswered and, indeed, the inconsistencies he left unresolved). We might simply note that Anderson's observations here beg the question. It is one thing to say, for example, that English commercial agriculture presupposed the Flemish market for wool. It is quite another to explain how 'commercial agriculture' became *capitalist* agriculture, how the *possibility of trade* became not only the *actuality* but the *necessity* of *competitive production*, how market *opportunities* became market *imperatives*, how this specific kind of agriculture set in train the development of a capitalist *system*.

We can certainly say that the European trading system was a necessary condition of capitalism, but we cannot just assume that commerce and capitalism are one and the same, or that one passed into the other by a simple process of growth. Anderson has assumed the very thing that needs to be demonstrated, namely that commerce, or indeed production for the market (a widespread practice throughout much of recorded history), became capitalism by means of sheer expansion, which at some point achieved a critical mass. His argument, in other words, suffers from the very circularity that has always afflicted the commercialization model.

3

MARXIST ALTERNATIVES

What the transition debate left unexplained and unaddressed was how and in what circumstances producers became subject to market *imperatives*. The assumption always appeared to be that capitalism emerged when obstacles to the realization of market *opportunities* were removed. A further episode in the ongoing debate among Marxists, however, has taken up the challenge of the transition debate in an effort to explain the transition from feudalism to capitalism without reading capitalist principles back into pre-capitalist societies – without, that is, assuming the very thing that needs to be explained.

THE BRENNER DEBATE

Historian Robert Brenner initiated a debate in 1976 with an important article, 'Agrarian Class Structure and Economic Development in Pre-Industrial Europe', published in the journal *Past and Present*.[1] That article took aim at two influential models of historical explanation. The first was the increasingly dominant demographic model according to which economic development in post-medieval Europe followed long-term cycles in population growth – what he called a secular Malthusianism. The second was the commercialization model.

Brenner attacked the very foundations of both these competing models. In particular, he emphasized their inability to account for the fact that very different, indeed opposite, effects were produced in different countries by the same factors, with varying consequences not only for income distribution between classes but also for long-term economic growth and the development of productive forces. These divergent effects of apparently similar causes – similar demographic patterns in one model, insertion in the same network of increasing trade in the other – were enough to put in question the status of these causes as independent variables and seriously weakened the explanatory force of the dominant models.

In their place, Brenner offered a powerful alternative explanation for the unprecedented process of self-sustaining economic growth that established itself in early modern England. His explanation focused on the varying configurations of social property relations that determined the divergent effects, in different contexts, of other factors (whose importance he did not dismiss) such as demographic cycles or the expansion of trade.

Brenner was clearly influenced by Maurice Dobb and, in the terms of the original transition debate, he was clearly more on Dobb's side than on Sweezy's. At the same time, like Sweezy, he was troubled by certain aspects of Dobb's argument. In his effort to explain the origin of capitalism without assuming its prior existence, Brenner concluded that there was no already existing capitalism, even in embryonic form, to challenge feudalism – and this applied not only to pre-capitalist forms of trade but also to petty commodity production treated, in the manner of Dobb and Hilton, as a kind of proto-capitalism. Like Sweezy, he took as his starting point the tenacity of feudalism, criticizing other accounts of the transition for neglecting the 'internal logic and solidity' of pre-capitalist economies and for proceeding as if economic actors will adopt capitalist strategies when given the chance – a criticism that applies not only to the commercialization model but, in some ways, even to the theory of rising petty commodity production.

Brenner, however, did not, like Sweezy, proceed by looking

for some external impetus to the dissolution of feudalism (in the context of certain property relations, for example, trade could and did lead, he argued, to a *tightening*, rather than a loosening, of pre-capitalist property forms). Instead, like Dobb and Hilton, Brenner looked for a dynamic internal to feudalism. But here is the major difference between his approach and theirs: what he was explicitly looking for was an internal dynamic that did not presuppose an already existent capitalist logic.

Class struggle figures prominently in his argument, as it did in Dobb's and Hilton's, but with Brenner it is not a question of *liberating* an impulse toward capitalism. Instead, it is a matter of lords and peasants, in certain specific conditions peculiar to England, involuntarily setting in train a capitalist dynamic while acting, in class conflict with each other, to reproduce themselves *as they were*. The unintended consequence was a situation in which producers were subjected to market imperatives. So Brenner really did depart from the old model and its tendency to assume the very thing that needs to be explained.

Brenner's explanation has to do with the very specific conditions of English property relations, and he emphasizes not just the specificity of Europe in relation to other cases but the differences among various states in Europe. In other words, the distinctive conditions that, for example, Michael Mann attributes to Europe in general in the Middle Ages are, for Brenner, not enough to explain the development of capitalism, or the specificity of the process of self-sustaining economic growth that emerged in England. In fact, his argument makes it clear that the dissolution of feudalism had more than one outcome in Europe – in particular, capitalism in England and absolutism in France, an absolutism that was not, as it was for Perry Anderson, simply a transitional phase in a more or less unilinear path toward capitalism.

In England, an exceptionally large proportion of land was owned by landlords and worked by tenants whose conditions of tenure increasingly took the form of economic leases, with rents not fixed by law or custom but responsive to market conditions. It could even be said that there existed a market in leases. The conditions of tenure were such that growing numbers of tenants were subjected to market imperatives – not the *opportunity* to produce for the market and to grow from petty producers into capitalists but the *need* to specialize for the market and to produce competitively – simply in order to guarantee access to the means of subsistence and to the land itself. This was in contrast to peasants, who, because they remained in direct possession of their means of subsistence, were shielded from competition and the compulsions of the market, even if they engaged in market exchange.

At the same time, landlords in England were also in a special position. Although they controlled a uniquely large proportion of the best land, they did not enjoy – and did not really need – the kinds of extra-economic powers on which, say, the French aristocracy depended for much of its wealth. The English ruling class was distinctive in its growing dependence on the *productivity* of tenants, rather than on exerting coercive power to squeeze more surplus out of them.

In other words, English property relations had what Brenner calls their own distinctive 'rules for reproduction'. Both direct producers and landlords came to depend on the market in historically unprecedented ways just to secure the conditions of their own self-reproduction. These rules produced their own distinctive laws of motion. The result was to set in train a new historical dynamic: an unprecented rupture with old Malthusian cycles, a process of self-sustaining development, new competitive pressures that had their own effects on the need to increase productivity, reconfiguring and further concentrating landhold-ing, and so on. This new dynamic is agrarian capitalism (which will be discussed in greater detail in Part II), and it was specific to England.

Although Brenner was clearly influenced by Dobb and Hilton, the difference between his argument and theirs should by now be clear. The operative principle in his argument is compulsion or imperative, not opportunity. If, for example, the petty commodity producer or yeoman farmer plays a major role here, it is not as the agent of an opportunity but as the subject of an imperative. Yeomen were typically the very kind of capitalist tenants who were subject to competitive pressures, and even owner-occupiers would be subject to those pressures once the competitive productivity of agrarian capitalism set the terms of economic survival. Both landlords and tenants came to depend on success in the market, as the former relied on the profits of the latter for their rents. Both had an interest in agricultural 'improvement', the enhancement of productivity by means of innovative land use and techniques, which often implied, among other things, enclosure – not to mention the increasing exploitation of wage labour.

In a sense, Brenner also answered Sweezy's question about the 'really revolutionary way'. The capitalist tenant in England was not just a petty producer who had grown into a capitalist. His specific relation to the means of production, the conditions in which he had access to land itself, in a sense made him a capitalist *from the start* – that is, he became a capitalist not just because he had grown to some appropriate size or level of prosperity, not even just because his relative wealth allowed him to employ wage labour (non-capitalist farmers even in the ancient world were known to employ wage labour), but because his relations to the means of his own self-reproduction from the outset subjected him, together with any wage labourers he may have employed, to market imperatives.

There have been various criticisms of Brenner, and some of the local disagreements about specific historical points are no doubt well taken. But let me just briefly outline some of the more general criticisms that have implications for the larger issues in the transition debate.

Brenner's critique of earlier explanations had been, above all, that they took as given precisely those features of capitalism that require explanation, invoking, in circular fashion, some kind of

pre-existing capitalism in order to explain the *emergence* of capitalism. The criticisms levelled against him in *The Brenner Debate*
tended to repeat that mistake, not really defending so much as
simply reproducing the presuppositions he had challenged. His
critics, including both demographic historians and some Marxists,
argued against him from a vantage point that took for granted the
very aspects of capitalism he had sought to explain.

So, for example, the dean of demographic historians, Emmanuel Le Roy Ladurie, attacked Brenner for conflating economic
and political factors by talking about 'surplus-extracting' classes
and 'ruling' classes as if they were one and the same. A Marxist
historian, Guy Bois, took exception to the 'voluntarism' of
Brenner's 'political Marxism', which, he maintained, neglected
economic factors altogether. The latter account of Brenner's
argument seemed to be reinforced in the introduction to the
volume by R. H. Hilton, who (in diplomatic and more or less
coded disagreement with Brenner) presented the issue between
the varieties of Marxism represented respectively by Bois and
Brenner as having to do with the relative weight given to *forces* as
distinct from *relations* of production, the '*whole* mode of production' as distinct from just class conflict, economic factors as distinct
from simply political ones. Hilton, despite his own tremendous
contribution to the history of class struggle, seemed to be hinting
that Brenner had leaned too much in the 'politicist' direction.

The criticisms levelled by Bois and Le Roy Ladurie were quite
substantially beside the point, and both were criticizing Brenner
from a vantage point that took for granted a separation between
the 'political' and the 'economic' that is specific to capitalism.
Brenner's whole argument was predicated on the important
observation, proposed originally by Marx, that pre-capitalist
societies were characterized by 'extra-economic' forms of surplus
extraction, carried out by means of political, juridical, and military
power, or what Brenner now calls 'politically constituted property'. In such cases, direct producers – notably peasants, who
remained in possession of the means of production – were

compelled by the superior force of their overlords to give up some of their surplus labour in the form of rent or tax. In the case of European feudalism in particular, lordship (as we saw in the discussion of Anderson) represented a *unity* of political and economic power. This is in sharp contrast to capitalism, where surplus extraction is purely 'economic', achieved through the medium of commodity exchange as propertyless workers, responding to purely 'economic' coercions, sell their labour power for a wage in order to gain access to the means of production. Following this insight to its logical conclusion, Brenner was neither, as Le Roy Ladurie complained, simplistically amalgamating economic and political factors, nor, as Bois maintained, 'privileging' political as against economic factors in his explanation of the transition from feudalism. Instead, he was exploring the consequences of the *fusion* of the 'economic' and the 'political', the unity of 'surplus-extracting' and 'ruling' classes, which was, precisely, a constitutive feature of the feudal mode of production.

Nor was it a matter of neglecting the technical forces of production. Brenner was simply explicating the fundamental difference between the capitalist mode of appropriation, which depends on improving labour productivity because of the imperatives of competition and profit maximization – and hence encourages the improvement of productive forces – and pre-capitalist modes of appropriation, where no such imperatives existed. These earlier modes were not driven by the same requirement to improve the productivity of labour, because surplus appropriation by dominant classes depended not on increasing the productivity of the direct producers but on strengthening the appropriator's coercive power to squeeze more surplus labour out of the producers. Brenner's principal questions, then, were these: how was it that old forms of 'politically constituted property' were replaced in England by a purely 'economic' form, and how did this set in train a distinctive pattern of self-sustaining economic development?

Since *The Brenner Debate*, other criticisms have surfaced. First, there is a general criticism of the very idea that English agrarian relations were distinctive enough – in the seventeenth or even the eighteenth century – to justify calling them agrarian capitalism. There are two different kinds of arguments against the idea of agrarian capitalism. One has to do with whether English economic growth really was distinctive, whether, in particular, English agriculture even in the *eighteenth* century was distinct, specifically in its drive to improve productivity. Why, for example, some critics have asked, was French agricultural productivity in the eighteenth century roughly equivalent to that of English agriculture?[2] The second objection has to do with wage labour: since capitalism is defined, above all, by the exploitation of wage labour, some critics say, is it not a decisive argument against the concept of agrarian capitalism – or at least against its existence in the seventeenth century – that England was not yet a predominantly wage-earning society, that permanent and regular wage labourers were still very much in the minority?[3] What about the processes of expropriation and proletarianization, the differentiation of the English peasantry into prosperous farmers, on the one hand, and a propertyless class, on the other? Do these processes not belong to the *pre*-history of capitalism?

The first objection – about agricultural productivity in France – misses the point. It turns out that what these critics mean is that French agricultural production in the eighteenth century achieved total outputs and/or land-productivity roughly equivalent to English agriculture. But consider the fact that it took fewer people in England than in France to produce the same outputs – so that England could, for example, feed a proportionately larger urban population with fewer people engaged in agricultural production. This means that the so-called 'equivalence' of French and English productivity, far from challenging the distinctiveness of English property relations and agrarian capitalism, actually confirms it. These same distinctive conditions created both a potential non-agricultural labour force and a potential mass market for the most basic necessities and cheap consumer goods, which were essential conditions for the development of *industrial* capitalism.

How, then, is Brenner's argument affected by the other question, about the extent of wage labour? The problem here is not only an empirical one. We can agree that the extent of wage labour was limited in early modern England, especially regular and permanent – as distinct from casual or seasonal – wage labour. And we can agree that the process of expropriation and proletarianization was, by definition, absolutely central to the story of capitalism. But here, too, there is a begging of the question, and here again Brenner sets out to explain what others have taken for granted.

Brenner does not assume that a pre-existing division between rich and poor peasants such as has existed at other times and places would inevitably lead to polarization into rich farmers and dispossessed labourers. For example, both England and France in the later fifteenth century possessed a middle peasantry with relatively large holdings. (It might be added here that even in the sixteenth century, agricultural productivity in the two cases was not yet clearly different either.) Yet from this common starting point, they diverged in substantially different historical directions, the French toward increasing morcellization of peasant holdings, the English toward the agrarian triad of landlord, capitalist tenant, and wage labourer; the English toward agricultural improvement, the French toward agricultural stagnation.

Brenner has been accused of neglecting the role of small and middling farmers in the rise of capitalism and of writing a history of capitalism 'from above'.[4] But in his argument, it is neither landlords nor middling farmers nor, indeed, any other single class whose agency explains the rise of capitalism. It is rather a particular system of class *relations*, within which the participants acted to reproduce themselves *as they were*, with the unintended consequence of setting off a process of development that gave rise to capitalism.

It is certainly true, as some Marxist historians have argued, that the development of English capitalism required the development of fairly prosperous 'middling' farmers and that yeomen played a leading role in the history of capitalism. It is, however, another matter to suggest that, once small commodity producers had thrown off the feudal fetters preventing them from growing into larger commodity producers prosperous enough to employ wage labour, the advent of capitalism was more or less guaranteed. This is where Brenner departs from his predecessors. The first point that comes immediately to mind here is that richer peasants have existed at many times and in many places, without becoming capitalists. Thus it must be asked why richer peasants in England began to behave in ways substantially different from any other prosperous peasants throughout recorded history, why English yeomen were not like Russian kulaks, or indeed like large tenant farmers in France at the same time. That difference, and the reasons for it, are precisely what Brenner has sought to explain.

Brenner does not assume that the English ruling class could simply have expropriated small farmers by brute force, or that they would have done so even if they could, in the absence of very specific economic conditions that made the dispossession of small producers not only possible but also profitable. Brenner's explanation of the differentiation of the English peasantry (the 'rise of the yeoman'), which eventually ended in a polarization between capitalist farmers and propertyless labourers, has to do with the new economic logic that subjected English farmers to the imperatives of competition in unprecedented ways and degrees. This logic was imposed on farmers whether or not they consistently employed wage labour. It applied even when the tenant was himself, or together with his family, the direct producer. The effect was to increase the pressures on less productive farmers and to drive them off the land, while more successful farmers acquired more land. In that sense, the differentiation of the peasantry was more effect than cause of the new property relations.

This is a particularly important point: Brenner makes it clear that direct producers could be deprived of non-market access to the means of their own self-reproduction even while remaining in possession of the means of production, and that such a condition subjected them to the demands of the market. To reiterate the indispensable contrast we have been drawing here: peasants elsewhere and at other times had availed themselves of market *opportunities*, but English farmers were distinctive in their degree of subjection to market *imperatives*.

Brenner set out to explain why and how this came to be so; how producers were deprived of non-market access to the means of their self-reproduction and even to land itself; how landlordly forms of exploitation were transformed from 'extra-economic' surplus extraction to the appropriation of capitalist rents; how it came about that both landlords and tenants were compelled and enabled to move in response to the imperatives of competition; how new forms of appropriation established new compulsions; and how those compulsions conditioned the differentiation – and in large part the dispossession – of the peasantry. This happened through purely 'economic' pressures of competition no less than through more direct coercion by landlords with a new kind of economic interest in large and concentrated holdings. A mass proletariat was the *end*, not the beginning, of the process. It cannot be emphasized enough that for Brenner, the market dependence of economic actors was a *cause*, not a result, of proletarianization.

Brenner goes further than previous Marxist accounts in explaining the specificity of capitalism, especially in his argument that the distinctive dynamics of capitalism come into play when producers become market-dependent, and therefore subject to the imperatives of competition, which happens even without their complete separation from the means of production, when their access to the means of subsistence becomes dependent on the market. This has important theoretical implications for our understanding of capitalism in general, as well as for our understanding of capitalist history. The great strength of Brenner's historical argument is that it emphasizes the specificity of the process that brought capitalism into being, with its new and historically specific economic logic, and that he makes a convincing effort to explain how it came about. Many historians have claimed to be explaining the transition from feudalism to capitalism. But in their various ways, most attempts to explain the process of transition tend to generalize laws of motion specific to capitalism and turn them into universal principles of historical movement. Even when such attempts acknowledge the particularity of capitalism as a specific historical form, the emergence of that historical form takes place by means of essentially capitalist processes. In that sense, there is no transition. Brenner is one of a very few writers who actually do deal with a *process* of transition, the transformation of one kind of society into another, one set of rules for reproduction into another, one historical dynamic into another.

BRENNER AND 'BOURGEOIS REVOLUTION'

One final criticism of Brenner is especially revealing. Some years after the original Brenner debate, Brenner published *Merchants and Revolution* (1993), a major study of early modern England that considered the role of merchants in the English Revolution. Several critics quickly seized on the fact that Brenner was attributing an important revolutionary role to merchants. After insisting that capitalism was born in the countryside, they argued, Brenner has had to acknowledge the bourgeoisie and bourgeois revolution after all.

Among the foremost exponents of this view was Perry Anderson. There is, he argued in a review of the book, a 'deep paradox' in Brenner's work, a fundamental contradiction between his original thesis on the origin of capitalism and his latest work on merchants:

Here, if ever, were revolutionary bourgeois. The species declared a fiction in France was *bel et bien* a reality in England, a hundred years before the Convention. There is a nice irony that it should be massive historical evidence, running against – not with – a theoretical conviction which has brought a Marxist scholar to this conclusion. The detractor of the significance of merchant capital in principle has been the first to establish, in spell-binding detail, its role as a demi-urge in practice.[5]

Brenner, it must first be said, has conceded nothing of the kind. But to understand the significance of his argument, we need to situate it in the context of his views on 'bourgeois revolution'. There is no question that he has issued a challenge to conventional Marxist historiography on this score, strongly suggesting that its conception of bourgeois revolution has much in common with the commercialization model.

The traditional conception of bourgeois revolution, he argued, belongs to a phase of Marx's work still heavily dependent upon the mechanical materialism of the eighteenth-century Enlightenment and contrasts sharply with Marx's mature critique of political economy.[6] In the earlier theory, productive forces develop almost naturally via the division of labour, which in turn evolves in response to expanding markets, so that the pre-existence of capitalism is invoked in order to explain its coming into being. The traditional conception of bourgeois revolution as an account of the transition to capitalism is, then, self-contradictory and self-defeating, because on its own assumptions, it renders revolution doubly unnecessary.

> First, there is no *transition* to accomplish, really: since the model starts with bourgeois society in the towns, foresees its evolution taking place by way of bourgeois mechanisms, and has feudalism transcend itself in consequence of its exposure to trade, the problem of how one type of society is transformed into another is simply assumed away and never posed. Second, since bourgeois society self-develops and dissolves feudalism, the bourgeois revolution can hardly claim a necessary role.[7]

Brenner was arguing that the thesis of bourgeois revolution, like the old commercialization model, assumed the very thing that needed to be explained by attributing to the bourgeoisie a capitalist rationality that had only to be released from the bonds of feudalism. In this way, he opened the way for a thorough reassessment of the bourgeoisie and its role in the rise of capitalism. This is the background to his account of London merchants, and especially the book's lengthy postscript. The charge that he has undermined his own original thesis simply replicates the circular and question-begging logic that that thesis was designed to correct.

The point is nowhere better illustrated than in Perry Anderson's 'deep paradox'. His criticism, it can be argued, is every bit as question-begging as the old commercialization model, and it draws our attention to one very important consequence of that model: the long-standing tendency to equate 'bourgeois' with 'capitalist'.

We may be utterly convinced that, say, the French Revolution was thoroughly bourgeois, indeed much more so than the English, without coming a flea-hop closer to determining whether it was also *capitalist*. As long as we accept that there is no necessary identification of *bourgeois* (or *burgher* or *city*) with *capitalist*, the revolutionary bourgeois can be far from a fiction, even – or especially – in France, where the model revolutionary bourgeois was not a capitalist or even an old-fashioned merchant but a lawyer or officeholder. At the same time, if the revolutionary bourgeois in England was inextricably linked with capitalism, it is precisely because capitalist social property relations had already been established in the English countryside.

There is, of course, much that Brenner does not do. One especially important point demanding exploration is that, although the commercialization model may be fatally flawed, capitalism did emerge within a network of international trade and could not have emerged without that network. So a great deal still needs to be said about how England's particular insertion into the European trading system determined the development of English capitalism. England arguably transformed the nature of trade by creating a distinctively integrated *national* market (centred on London), perhaps the first truly competitive market. Much still needs to be learned about how this affected the nature of *international* trade.

To understand how English capitalism differed from, and also transformed, the nature of trade in Europe and elsewhere, we also need to understand the nature of non-capitalist trade. If the commercialization model is to be effectively challenged, it is important to account for the patterns of development associated with commercialization that did *not* give rise to capitalism. In the next chapter, there will be some observations on this question and a brief sketch of societies that achieved high levels of commercialization and technological advance without setting in motion the imperatives of capitalist development.

Another big issue is the European state system and its contribution to the development of English capitalism. Together, the system of trade and the state system operated as the conduit through which England was eventually able to transmit its competitive pressures to other states and economies, so that *non*-capitalist states could become engines of capitalist development in response to these external pressures, geopolitical and military as well as commercial.[8] We have hardly begun to explore the mechanisms by which capitalism imposed its imperatives on other European states, and eventually on the whole world. This would also have to play a major part in explaining how capitalism transformed traditional forms of colonialism into a new, capitalist form of imperialism. These issues will be taken up in Chapters 7 and 8. A systematic exploration of these historical questions might, among other things, be a big help in dealing with the so-called 'globalization' process today.

E. P. THOMPSON

Brenner's argument, by showing how direct producers became subject to market imperatives, even if it does not explicate the role of towns and markets in the development of capitalism, explains the context in which the very nature of trade and markets was transformed, acquiring an entirely new economic role and a new systemic logic. This happened long before industrialization and was a precondition of it. Market imperatives, in other words, imposed themselves on direct producers before the mass proletarianization of the workforce. They were a decisive factor in creating a mass proletariat, as market forces, supported by direct coercion in the form of political and judicial intervention, created a propertyless majority.

How 'market society' established itself in the period leading up to industrialization has been most vividly described by E. P. Thompson. In his work, the establishment of market society comes to life not only as a process of proletarianization, particularly in his classic work *The Making of the English Working Class* (1963), but also as a living confrontation between market society and alternative practices and values. The implantation of market society emerges as a confrontation between classes, between those whose interests were expressed in the new political economy of the market and those who contested it by putting the right of subsistence before the imperatives of profit.

In the central section of *The Making of the English Working Class* entitled 'Exploitation', Thompson outlines what for him are the pivotal moments in the emergence of industrial capitalism. Two related points stand out in his analysis. The first is the timing of the transformative moment, the 'making' of a new working class. Thompson situates the transforming experience of the English working class, the process in which a new proletariat and a new working-class culture were forged, in the period 1790–1832. His analysis therefore ends well before the industrial transformation of production was complete or even very far

advanced. The second, related point is that he sees a transformation in what appears to be a fundamental continuity: even
workers who, on the face of it, seem hardly different from their
artisanal predecessors, and whose oppositional culture is still
deeply rooted in old pre-industrial popular and radical traditions,
are, for Thompson, a 'fresh race of beings', a new kind of
proletariat.

Some Marxist critics of Thompson have interpreted these
striking features as evidence of Thompson's preoccupation with
'subjective', cultural factors, at the expense of 'objective' changes
in the mode of production itself, specifically the transformative
effects of technological change on the organization of production
and on the nature of the labour force.[9] But here again, Marxist
critics may be conceding too much to standard histories of
capitalist development. The tendency among historians of various
ideological persuasions has been to trace the causes of the 'Industrial Revolution' – if they accept the notion of an industrial
revolution at all – to technical innovations or developments in
trade and market relations. Thompson, by contrast, like Brenner
after him, is doing something rather more subtle and complex –
following, it can be argued, the principles (if not always the
practice) of Marx himself. For all the many differences in style
and subject matter between Brenner and Thompson, it is possible to imagine an account of industrialization building upon
Brenner's challenge to conventional ideas about capitalist development that would have more in common with Thompson's
history than with any other.

Brenner, readers will remember, sought to account for the
emergence of new 'rules for reproduction'. He showed that the
dynamic of self-sustaining growth, and the constant need for
improvement in labour productivity, presupposed transformations
in property relations that created a need for such improvements
simply to permit the principal economic actors – landlords and
peasants – to reproduce themselves. The divergences between
England and France, for example, had little to do in the first

instance with any differences in their respective technological capacities. They were distinguished by the nature of relations between landlords and peasants: one case demanded enhancement of labour-productivity, the other did not and in some ways even impeded the development of productive forces. The systematic drive to revolutionize the forces of production was result more than cause.

Thompson's account of industrialization is rooted in the same perception. His purpose is to explore the consequences of specifically capitalist modes of exploitation. Among those consequences in the period of transition to industrial capitalism was the intensification of labour and work discipline. What created the drive to intensify exploitation was not the emergence of steam or the factory system but rather the need inherent in capitalist property relations to increase productivity and profit. Those capitalist imperatives were imposed on traditional forms of work no less than on new forms of labour, on artisans still engaged in pre-industrial production no less than on factory hands. 'Large-scale sweated outwork', Thompson argues, 'was as intrinsic to this revolution as was factory production and steam.'[10] A common experience of capitalist imperatives and capitalist exploitation is what made it possible for diverse kinds of workers to join in class organizations and create a new kind of working-class culture. To be sure, these imperatives were bound to transform the organization of production and the nature of the working class, but the factory system was result more than cause.

Here Thompson is pursuing the distinction made by Marx between the 'formal' and the 'real' subsumption of labour by capital. In the first instance, capital appropriated surplus labour from workers still engaged in traditional forms of production. This form of exploitation was driven by capitalist imperatives, its compulsions of competition and accumulation, but those imperatives did not at first transform the technical process of production. We may want to say that capitalism did not reach maturity until capital had transformed the labour process itself specifically to meet the needs of capital – that is, until capitalism assumed its industrial form. But we can nonetheless recognize that industrial capitalism was the result, not the cause, of capitalist laws of motion.

So the answer to those like Perry Anderson who have wondered why Thompson, after *The Making of the English Working Class*, moved back into the eighteenth century instead of forward, beyond the 1830s to a fuller account of industrialization, is that he was trying to explain the establishment of *capitalism* as a social form, not some neutral technical process called 'industrialization'. He was particularly interested in the eighteenth century as the moment when the capitalist transformation of property relations was being consolidated and was playing itself out in the articulation of a new capitalist ideology more self-conscious and explicit than ever before. It was also a moment when the new economic principles had not yet taken full shape as a hegemonic ideology, the political economy of the market, which would soon infiltrate even some of the most radical opposition to capitalism.

Thompson suggests that in eighteenth-century England the market was in fact the main arena of struggle. This was so for reasons very specific to this transitory moment in English history. On the one hand, this was a moment of 'free' labour, subject neither to pre-capitalist, extra-economic forms of domination nor as yet, in general, to the new disciplines of the factory, so that people for a short time still controlled 'their own immediate relations and modes of work'. On the other hand, 'they had very little control over the market for their products or over the prices of raw materials or food'. This is why social protest was so often directed at the market. People, often women, opposed not only unjust prices but also illegitimate and immoral market practices – practices designed to increase profit, which from the vantage point of market society and capitalist rationality seem perfectly normal today but which violated certain customary expectations about rights of access to the means of life.[11]

In some of these protests, we can also see opposition to the transformation of the market from a visible, more or less trans-parent, institution into an 'invisible hand'. The market that people were most familiar with was a physical place where some put commodities on offer for others to buy, according to principles governed to some extent by custom, communal regulation, and expectations about the right to subsistence. Now it was becoming a mechanism beyond communal control, as the transparency of market transactions was supplanted by the mysteries of a 'self-regulating' market, the price mechanism, and the subordination of all communal values to the imperatives of profit.

Thompson also shows how the new ideology of political economy, including new conceptions of property and the ethic of profit, was increasingly enforced by state repression. The courts would put the proprietor's right to profit by increasing productiv-ity above other kinds of right, such as the customary use rights long enjoyed by non-owners, or the right to subsistence. And the civil authority reacted more violently, especially in the wake of the French Revolution, to protest against unjust prices and market practices. Coercion by the state, in other words, was required to impose the coercion of the market.

SUMMING UP

So far the argument of this book has been that the main problem in most standard histories of capitalism is that they start – and end – with assumptions that obscure the specificity of capitalism. We need a form of history that brings this specificity into sharp relief, one that acknowledges the difference between commercial profit-taking and capitalist accumulation, between the market as an opportunity and the market as an imperative, and between transhistorical processes of technological development and the specific capitalist drive to improve labour productivity. We need to trace these specificities of capitalism to their roots in forms of social property and class relations. Most Marxists would no doubt claim to be doing all or most of these things, but I have tried to show that their accounts of history with very few exceptions fail to proceed consistently on that basis, with the consequence that the specificity of capitalism remains disguised.

On the face of it, much has happened in historical scholarship since the commercialization model first emerged. Some of the most well-established conventions of Western historiography have been challenged and ostensibly subverted at their very foundations – not only by Marxists but also by 'revisionist' historians of one kind or another, postmodernists and other iconoclasts. Yet it is a measure of how deeply rooted the old question-begging explanations of capitalism are that they are still present in the most current scholarship – not only in anti-Eurocentric critiques but also in today's conceptions of modernity and postmodernity – and in our conventional everyday language, which still identifies *capitalist* with *bourgeois*, and both with modernity.

PART II

The Origin of Capitalism

4

COMMERCE OR CAPITALISM?

The 'transition from feudalism to capitalism' is typically treated as a general European – or at least Western European – process. Yet European feudalism in Europe was internally diverse, and it produced several different outcomes, only one of which was capitalism.

It is not just a matter of different rates of 'combined and uneven development' or even of different transitional phases. The autonomous city-states that prospered in medieval and Renaissance Italy, for example, or the absolutist state in France, were distinct formations, each with its own internal logic of process that need not have given rise to capitalism. Where and when they did issue in capitalism, it was only as they came within the orbit of an already existing capitalist system and the competitive pressures it was able to impose on its political, military, or commercial rivals. No entry into the capitalist economy could thereafter be the same as earlier ones, as they all became subject to a larger and increasingly international capitalist system.[1]

The tendency to take for granted that capitalism was an inevitable, if antagonistic, outgrowth of European feudalism is, as we have seen, rooted in the conviction that the autonomous town that grew within the interstices of feudalism's 'parcellized sovereignties' was not only the natural enemy that would destroy the feudal system but also the 'cuckoo's egg' within it that would give birth to capitalism. To detach ourselves from that presupposition means, first, to disentangle *capitalist* from *bourgeois*, and *capitalism* from the *city*.

TOWNS AND TRADE

The association of capitalism with cities is one of the most well-established conventions of Western culture. Capitalism is supposed to have been born and bred in the city. But more than that, the implication is that *any* city, with its characteristic practices of trade and commerce, is by its very nature potentially capitalist from the start, and only extraneous obstacles have stood in the way of *any* urban civilization giving rise to capitalism. Only the wrong religion, the wrong kind of state, or other ideological, political, or cultural fetters tying the hands of urban classes have prevented capitalism from springing up anywhere and everywhere, since time immemorial, or at least since technology has permitted the production of adequate surpluses.

What accounts for the development of capitalism in the West, according to this view, is the unique autonomy of its cities and of their quintessential class, the burghers or bourgeois. In other words, capitalism emerged in the West less because of what was present than because of what was absent: constraints on urban economic practices. In those conditions, it took only a more or less natural expansion of trade to trigger the development of capitalism to its full maturity. All that was needed was a quantitative growth, and the accumulation of wealth that came with it, which occurred almost inevitably with the passage of time (in some versions, of course, helped along, but not originally caused, by the 'Protestant ethic').

There is much that is questionable in these assumptions about the natural connection between cities and capitalism, but above all the tendency to naturalize capitalism, to disguise its distinctiveness as a historically specific social form with a beginning and, potentially, an end. The tendency to identify capitalism with cities and urban commerce has, as we have seen, generally been accompanied by an inclination to make capitalism appear a more or less automatic consequence of practices as old as human history, or even the consequence of a 'natural' inclination, in Adam Smith's words, to 'truck, barter, and exchange'.

Yet there have, throughout history, been a great many towns and a great deal of trade that never gave rise to capitalism. For that matter, there have been elaborate urban settlements – such as the temple cities of ancient empires – that have not been commercial centres. More particularly, there have been societies with advanced urban cultures, highly developed trading systems, and far-flung commercial networks that have made ample use of market *opportunities* but have not systematically experienced what we have been calling market *imperatives*.

These commercial powers have often produced a rich material and cultural infrastructure, far in advance of developments in the European backwater that first gave rise to capitalism. No reasonable person would deny that, in Asia, Africa, and the Americas, there were 'high' civilizations, which in some cases developed commercial practices, as well as technological advances of various kinds, that far surpassed those of medieval England. But the emergence of capitalism is difficult to explain precisely because it bears no relation to prior superiority or more advanced development in commercial sophistication, science and technology, or 'primitive accumulation' in the classical sense of material wealth.

Nor was the autonomy of cities the decisive factor. Free urban communes in Europe may have provided fertile ground for trade, prosperous burghers, and urban patriciates, but there is no obvious correlation between the success of such autonomous commercial centres and the rise of capitalism. Vastly successful commercial city-states like Florence did not give rise to capitalism, while capitalism did emerge in England, whose cities, in the context of a precociously centralized monarchical state, were arguably among the least autonomous in Europe.

The critical factor in the divergence of capitalism from all other forms of 'commercial society' was the development of certain social property relations that generated market imperatives and capitalist 'laws of motion', which imposed themselves on production. The great non-capitalist commercial powers had producing classes and especially peasants who remained in possession of their means of subsistence, and land in particular. They were ruled and exploited by dominant classes and states that relied on 'extra-economic' appropriation or 'politically constituted property' of various kinds. These great civilizations were not systematically subjected to the pressures of competitive production and profit-maximization, the compulsion to reinvest surpluses, and the relentless need to improve labour-productivity associated with capitalism.

In the next chapter, we shall explore more closely the social property relations that did produce the imperatives of capitalist development. But first, to delineate the difference between capitalism and non-capitalist commerce, even at its most advanced and prosperous, let us look, in very general outline, at the logic of pre-capitalist trade.[2]

The simple logic of trade is 'the exchange of reciprocal requirements'. This can take place within a single community or among adjacent communities, and this simple logic can still operate where the direct exchange of products is replaced by circulation of commodities mediated by money. It does not by itself generate the need to maximize profit and, even less, to produce competitively. Beyond such simple acts of exchange, there are more complex transactions between separate markets, involving commercial profit-taking (buying cheap in one market and selling dear in another) in the process of conveyance from one market to another or arbitrage between them. This kind of trade may have a logic different from the simple exchange of reciprocal requirements, at least to the extent that requirements of commercial profit intervene. But here too there is no inherent and systematic compulsion to transform production.

Even in pre-capitalist societies, there are, of course, people who live by profit-taking, people who make a living by profitable trade. But the logic of non-capitalist production does not change simply because profit-seeking middlemen, even highly developed merchant classes, intervene. Their strategies need have nothing to do with transforming production in the sense required by capitalist competition. Profit by means of carrying trade or arbitrage between markets has strategies of its own. These do not depend on transforming production, nor do they promote the development of the kind of integrated market that imposes competitive imperatives. On the contrary, they thrive on fragmented markets and movement between them, rather than competition within a single market; and the links between production and exchange may be very tenuous.

The trading networks of medieval and early modern Europe, for instance, depended on a degree of local or regional specialization that allowed merchants to profit by carrying goods from one locale, where they were produced, to others, where they were not, or not in adequate quantities – to say nothing of their ventures much further afield, in a growing network of long-distance trade. But here as elsewhere in the non-capitalist world, though profit-seeking was a common and highly developed activity, it was separate from, if not actually opposed to, 'efficient' production.

Fierce commercial rivalries certainly existed, both between major economic powers and even within them, among their cities and local merchants. There were even major wars over trade. But these rivalries generally had less to do with competitive production of the capitalist kind than with 'extra-economic' factors such as superior shipping, domination of the seas and other transport routes, monopoly privileges, or highly developed financial institutions and instruments of arbitrage, typically supported by military force. Some of these extra-economic advantages, such as those in shipping or, indeed, military superiority, certainly depended on technological innovations, but this was not a matter of a systematic need to lower the costs of production in order to prevail in price competition.

Even later than the seventeenth century, most of the world, including Europe, was free of market imperatives. A vast system of trade certainly existed, extending across the globe. But nowhere, neither in the great trading centres of Europe nor in the vast commercial networks of the non-European world, was economic activity and production in particular driven by the imperatives of competition and accumulation. The dominant principle of trade everywhere was not surplus value derived from production but 'profit on alienation', 'buying cheap and selling dear'.

International trade is the economic activity that above all created the great commercial centres, which are, according to all versions of the commercialization model, supposed to have been the precursors of capitalism. This was essentially carrying trade, with merchants buying goods in one location to be sold for a profit in another, or 'commercial arbitrage between separate markets'.[3] But even within a single, powerful, and relatively unified European kingdom like France, basically the same principles of non-capitalist commerce prevailed. There was no single and unified market, a market in which people made profit not by buying cheap and selling dear, not by carrying goods from one market to another, but by producing more cost-effectively in direct competition with others in the same market.

The trade that created great commercial power tended to be in luxury goods, or at least goods destined for more prosperous households or answering to the needs and consumption patterns of dominant classes. There was no mass market for cheap everyday consumer products such as the market that would later drive industrial capitalism in Britain. Peasant producers typically produced not only their own food but also other everyday goods like clothing. There was, to be sure, a market in food, and peasants might take their surpluses to local markets, where the proceeds could be exchanged for other commodities. Farm produce might even be sold in markets further afield, and commerce particularly in grain was very extensive, especially to supply urban populations. But here again, the principles of trade were basically the same as in manufactured goods, with profits deriving from advantage in the processes of circulation more than from cost-effective and competitive production.

The kind of trade in luxury goods for a fairly limited market did not in itself carry a systematic impulse to improve productivity. But, as we shall see in a moment, it was not unique in this respect. Even trade in basic necessities like grain was governed by the same principles of profit in circulation rather than production – and, for that matter, its development was dependent on commerce in luxury goods. In all kinds of trade, the main vocation of the large merchant was circulation rather than production, and the main commercial advantages were 'extra-economic'.

Even when a major commercial centre like Florence – a case to which we shall return – developed domestic urban production (largely the production of luxury goods for a relatively limited market), in addition to its role in servicing external mercantile activity, the basic logic of economic transactions was not essentially different. It was still a matter of recycling wealth or 'profit on alienation' in the process of circulation, rather than the creation of value in production, and the appropriation of surplus value, in the capitalist manner.

These non-capitalist principles of trade existed in conjunction with non-capitalist modes of exploitation. For instance, in Western Europe, even where feudal serfdom had effectively disappeared, other forms of 'extra-economic' exploitation still prevailed. Even monetary rents in pre-capitalist societies were based on extra-economic power. In eighteenth-century France, for example, where peasants still constituted the vast majority of the population and remained in possession of most land, office in the central state served as an economic resource for many members of the dominant classes, as a means of extracting surplus labour in the form of taxes from peasant producers. Even rent-appropriating landlords typically depended on various extra-economic powers and privileges to enhance their wealth.

So peasants had direct access to the means of production, the land, while landlords and officeholders, with the help of various 'extra-economic' powers and privileges, extracted surplus labour from peasants directly in the form of rent or tax. While all kinds of people might buy and sell all kinds of things in the market, neither the peasant-proprietors who produced, nor the landlords and officeholders who appropriated what others produced, depended directly on the market for the conditions of their self-reproduction, and the relations between them were not mediated by the market.

It was, as we shall see in the next chapter, a fundamental change in these social property relations – a change that made producers, appropriators, and the relations between them market-dependent – that would bring about capitalism.

COMMERCE IN BASIC NECESSITIES

While much of the world's population since the emergence of agriculture has been devoted to the production of food, there have always been those who, for one reason or another and in various ways, have depended on others to produce it for them. The distribution of food from producers to non-producing consumers has taken many different forms, from gift-relationships or the obligations of kinship, to distribution by the state (as in the ancient Roman grain dole), to coercive appropriation by means of superior force of one kind or another. But trade in foodstuffs has obviously been a very widespread human practice. Control of the food supply has also been a major source of power and wealth, and merchants have grown rich by cornering such trade.

The commerce in food has ranged from local markets in which peasants have exchanged their surpluses for other commodities, to large-scale trade at greater distances, such as the massive

European trade in grain. But as widespread and ancient as the trade in food has been, its development into a major feature of social existence depended on the growth of cities, with large concentrations of people not engaged in the production of their own food.

In our exploration of the relation between capitalism and the city, and our critical examination of the 'commercialization model' of capitalist development, we can learn a great deal by scrutinizing the different ways in which the trade in food has figured in the larger economic scheme of things. It will be argued in the next chapter that capitalism was born when market imperatives seized hold of food production, the provision of life's most irreducible necessity. But before we reach that point, it might be useful, by way of contrast, to sketch out a different case, not one in which the market played no role or only a minor one but, on the contrary, one in which commerce was an essential condition of subsistence and social reproduction, yet where market imperatives were still not in play. We should not take for granted that extensive commerce even in the most basic necessities always carries with it the imperatives of competitive production, profit-maximization, and the relentless development of the productive forces.

In the commercialization model, international trade based in medieval and early modern Europe was supposed to be the foundation of capitalist development, so let us consider the role played here by trade in food. There was a well-established network of commerce in food, especially grain, that joined certain European food-producing regions with other parts of Europe unable to produce enough for their own consumption, particularly and mainly for people living in towns. A growing urban population in parts of the continent, and especially in the major commercial centres, created not only a growing market for luxury goods, supplied increasingly by long-distance trade beyond the borders of Europe, but also a market for very basic subsistence needs that their own domestic agriculture was unable to meet.

These needs were supplied above all by imported grain, especially from the Baltic region.

This trade in grain, a major feature of international trade, was conducted according to the principles of pre-capitalist commerce. Mercantile profit depended on bringing commodities from one market to another and was enhanced by the differences between the price of purchase in the producing regions and the price of sale in wealthy consuming regions. Grain could, for example, be bought cheap in the Baltic and sold relatively dear in the Dutch Republic (though cheap by local standards), whose merchants came to dominate the Baltic trade.

There is another sense, too, in which the grain trade bore the marks of pre-capitalist commerce. Imported grain was certainly an essential condition of commercial success in the major European trading powers, but the grain trade was not itself the motor of the European trading system, whose fortunes were always dependent on the fate of the luxury trade and the wealth of the prosperous consumers that impelled it. It is even possible to argue that the *need* for a massive trade in grain was determined by the luxurious consumption patterns of the wealthier classes, in the sense that the (grain-consuming) urban population of Europe was swelled by people servicing the opulent living and 'conspicuous consumption' of richer consumers.

In the Middle Ages, international trade was driven by the wealth of the landed aristocracy, whose consumption patterns – their hunger for luxuries, as well as for the instruments of 'extra-economic' coercion, especially military goods, on which their economic power depended – dictated the logic of the commercial system. 'The landed aristocracy,' writes Rodney Hilton,

> whether lay or ecclesiastical, constituted at all times the principal market for a range of products, mainly luxuries, which entered into international trade. . . . International trade, of course, dealt also in bulk commodities like grain and timber, but the demand for these was mainly urban and probably depended ultimately on the health of the international trade in luxuries.[4]

Even later, with the growth of towns and prosperous burgher classes, the same fundamental logic prevailed. Many more people, many of them poor, came to depend for their subsistence on cheap imported grain. But the international trading system of pre-capitalist Europe continued to be driven by the wealth and wants of prosperous consumers, as well as the needs of the state, not by the consumer needs and powers of those who entered the market above all to acquire the basic means of survival and self-reproduction, whether food or other commodities of everyday life, from inexpensive textiles to cheap cooking pots.

The point can be illustrated by considering the disjunction between commercial power in Europe and the trade in grain. The production and export of grain, as essential as it was to European subsistence, was not (until Britain broke the pattern) an index of wealth and economic power. It was even (as Marx once put it) the function of those 'left behind' in Europe's economic development. A division of labour developed between Europe's grain-exporting regions and its richest trading powers, such as the Dutch Republic. But this division of labour was never a simple exchange of necessities between specialized regions – grain from the Baltic for, say, the dairy products of the Low Countries. While the Dutch role in the Baltic grain trade was certainly paramount, commercial power such as theirs derived not simply from commerce in basic necessities but from trade in luxuries or relative luxuries consumed disproportionately by other rich commercial powers.

The commercial system of pre-capitalist Europe, then, was characterized by a series of disjunctions: the geographic separation between the production of grain and its consumption by countries whose wealth derived from trade in other commodities – not even necessarily from the *production* of those commodities but also, more particularly, from the conveyance, transshipment, and arbitrage of commodities produced elsewhere, and revenues from entrepôts. It is as commercial mediators more than as producers of traded commodities that the great commercial powers gained their huge wealth, and this was reflected in an imbalance between the production of basic necessities and economic power derived from trade in luxuries.

These disjunctions and imbalances were, needless to say, reinforced by the basic practicalities of transport and communication. The whole system, indeed, was based on the fragmentation of markets, detachment of one market from another, the distance between sites of production and sites of consumption, the geographic separation of supply and demand. Mercantile wealth depended precisely on the relative inaccessibility of markets and the possibility of profiting from an endless process of arbitrage between fragmented markets.

There was, then, a fundamental separation between consumption and production. The social conditions in which grain was produced in the exporting regions had very little to do with the conditions in which it was consumed in the rich commercial centres. This meant, among other things, that grain was cheap by the economic standards of the consuming powers, especially in the wealthy Dutch Republic, whose merchants and superior shipping dominated the Baltic trade, without the enhancement of productive forces in the producing regions. Nor did low costs in the grain-producing regions impose competitive pressures on the consuming economies that benefited from cheap imports. On the contrary, the costs of producing other commodities in those wealthy commercial economies were in effect reduced by access to such cheap basic 'inputs'. At any rate, the trading advantages of the commercial leaders did not depend primarily on competitive production but on 'extra-economic' factors such as monopoly privileges, superior shipping, sophisticated commercial practices and instruments, elaborate commercial networks, far-flung trading posts, and military might.

These disjunctions certainly meant that, while rich commercial nations may have been dependent on the grain trade for the means of survival, the cost of the most basic survival needs was disproportionately low in relation to the wealth derived from commerce in less necessary goods. But the same disjunctions also meant that the commercial centres whose wealth depended on them were vulnerable to the fragilities of the international trade in superfluous goods. Not only their great wealth but even their supply of cheap and basic necessities could suffer from declines in the luxury trade.

FLORENCE AND THE DUTCH REPUBLIC

Within the European trading system, there emerged several very successful and prosperous commercial centres that, according to the commercialization model, should have been the birthplaces of capitalism. In fact, according to some versions of the model, they were indeed capitalist, though for one reason or another their further development was thwarted and they never went the whole distance to industrial capitalism, until Britain led the way. These were the so-called 'failed transitions'.

No one could deny that in the great European commercial centres the wealth of the dominant classes rested on commerce, and that their appropriation of surpluses from direct producers did not here take the classic form of feudal rent. But here too, as in other pre-capitalist societies, great wealth still depended on politically constituted property; and here too this form of appropriation shaped the particular and self-limiting course of economic development.

Urban patriciates or merchant elites in commercial centres in medieval and early modern Europe often extracted great wealth from commercial activities, but they relied in large part on the privileges and powers associated with their status in the city. The success of these commercial centres, as we have seen, was dependent less on competitive production than on 'extra-economic' factors. Ruling elites in these centres depended on their civic status not only for privileged access to such extra-economic commercial advantages but typically also, as office-holders, for exploitation of domestic producers by means of direct extra-economic surplus extraction in the form of rents, dues, and taxes of one kind or another, so much so that cities of this kind have been described as collective lordships.

This is true even in cases like Florence, whose commercial wealth was based not only on trade in foreign goods but also on its own domestic products. Florence is a favourite with those preoccupied with 'failed transitions', because it was such a remarkably successful commercial power and also because of its dazzling cultural riches, as the quintessential home of the so-called 'Renaissance'. On any measure of commercial sophistication, domestic manufacture, or cultural achievement, Florence at that time far surpassed England, yet that northern backwater was then on the verge of its capitalist development, while the opulent Italian city-state 'failed' to take that route.

In relation to the surrounding countryside, the city of Florence was certainly a collective lordship, exploiting peasant producers in the *contado* no less than the absolutist state in France did its own peasants. At the same time, the success of Florentine trade in its own manufactured commodities continued to depend on extra-economic factors, on monopoly privileges, or on especially sophisticated commercial and financial practices (double-entry book-keeping is supposed to have originated there), which facilitated a commerce in goods whose success in a luxury market in any case had less to do with cost-effective production than with the skills of craftsmanship. Not the least significant trait of the Florentine economy was that its greatest commercial families, notably the Medici, moved into more lucrative non-productive enterprises, such as financial services for monarchs and popes, not to mention public office up to and including dynastic rule of the city-state itself.

As successful as such commercial centres were for a time, and as great as the wealth they amassed, their economic development was self-limiting. It is obviously true that the market played a central role in their development, but it seems just as clear that here it really did function more as an opportunity than as an imperative. At least, the market did not operate here in such a way as to create the relentless capitalist drive to maximize profit by developing the forces of production.

It may be possible to argue (as I would be inclined to do) that the non-capitalist character of such commercial economies was as much their strength as their weakness, and that, for instance, the Italian Renaissance, which flourished in the environment of commercial city-states in northern Italy like Florence, would not have achieved its great heights under the pressures of capitalist imperatives. But that is another story. The point here is simply that, in the absence of those imperatives, the pattern of economic development was bound to be different.

Where the necessary productive capacities were present, and the market, especially for luxury goods, was available, the dominant classes were willing and able to encourage and exploit not only commerce but also production. Merchants even organized and invested in production. Yet the appropriation of great wealth still depended on extra-economic powers and privileges, and far less on developing productive forces than on refining and extending the forces of appropriation. A system of this kind would inevitably respond to declining market opportunities not by enhancing labour-productivity and improving cost-effectiveness but by squeezing producers harder or by withdrawing altogether from production in favour of more 'extra-economic' powers of appropriation.

The case of the Dutch Republic in the sixteenth and seventeenth centuries is probably the most complex. It is the case for which the strongest argument can be made as a rival to England's claims as the first 'modern' or capitalist economy.[5] Its commercial wealth and cultural achievements were enormous. It pioneered some of the most sophisticated commercial practices and instruments, in banking, stock trading, and financial speculation, to say nothing of its technical capacities in shipping and its military successes. Even its technological development in enhancing productivity for a time exceeded all others in Europe, and the

English borrowed many of its agricultural advances. It had an exceptionally large urban population and seems to have been the most highly commercialized society in history, before the advent of capitalism. It was unusually dependent on trade to provide the most basic conditions of subsistence even for direct producers. More particularly, even its agricultural producers depended on trade to an unprecedented degree for basic subsistence needs, acquiring grain in the market by selling their own commodities, in particular dairy products. There can be no doubt that the great wealth of the Republic was founded on commerce, or that Dutch commercial elites invested in domestic production – notably in agriculture – in unprecedented ways and to an unprecedented degree.

For these reasons, the Dutch Republic is an even greater favourite than Florence as a 'failed transition', and many explanations have been offered for the fact that the Dutch did not take the leap to industrial capitalism as the English were to do. Some have put this down to the parasitic stranglehold of top-heavy cities, which, it is argued, eventually suppressed Dutch productivity, especially in agriculture, by squeezing it for rentier wealth. Others may emphasize the ways in which the cities did invest in production, and specifically productive agriculture, yet attribute the 'failed transition' to the Republic's dependence on the export market and hence on the larger European economy, which dragged the Dutch down with it when it went into decline. Yet another explanation is that the Dutch decline was just a typical secular downturn such as affects all 'modern' economies.

It could just be argued that, even when such explanations proceed from the premises of the commercialization model, they also tend to undermine it by treating the Republic's apparently *excessive* commercialization and urbanization as an obstacle to further development. But an alternative explanation might be that the Dutch 'failed' to follow the expected course of capitalist development because it was not in its essence a capitalist economy and was driven by a different economic logic. It is beyond the scope of this book to enter the debate about the Dutch economy. For our purposes, it is enough to point out some of the most important ways in which its pattern of development displayed the logic of a pre-capitalist economy.

The Dutch may have differed from other European powers in the extent to which they relied on the market even for their basic food supplies, but the commercial system in which they operated was still the pre-capitalist economy that characterized Europe as a whole. This is true not only in the sense that the Dutch were largely dependent on the European market, not least the market in luxury goods, and subject to its limitations, but also in the sense that the Dutch economy itself was dominated not by capitalist producers but by the commercial interests of merchants whose principal vocation, even when they invested in agriculture or industry, was circulation rather than production.

Perhaps the most important factor in the Dutch economy was the dominance of the city and the interests of urban elites, which also shaped the rural economy, not only as a large market for agricultural products but also as a source of investment. The great wealth and commercial power of the Republic depended disproportionately on its pre-eminence in international trade, conveying and marketing goods produced elsewhere. Without its leading role in international trade, and without the great wealth derived from Europe's growing luxury markets, the Dutch could not have developed either their huge urban population or, indeed, their productive agriculture. This was not so much a case in which agricultural productivity sustained an unusually large urban population (as would occur in England) but rather a case in which an unusually large urban population sustained by a dominant role in international trade, as a major link in the European commercial chain, also provided the conditions for a productive agriculture.

Despite its reliance on circulating goods produced elsewhere, the Republic did trade in its own domestic commodities. During the 'Golden Age', there was a substantial connection between Dutch commercial interests and domestic production, with urban

wealth ploughed into the countryside, most dramatically in massive land reclamation projects. But that connection between
commerce and production was, so to speak, always at one remove
and subject to disruption the moment the market for Dutch
products declined. The Dutch constructed their commercial
empire on the strength of other advantages outside the sphere of
production.

Nor is it clear that Dutch producers, and farmers in particular,
who were deeply engaged in production for the market, were subject
to the competitive imperatives we associate with capitalism. Here,
for example, the influence of low-cost grain-producing regions,
which benefited the Dutch even more than other economies, if
anything *reduced* competitive pressures by lowering the costs of
basic inputs, allowing Dutch farmers to produce and market their
own higher cost products, not basic grain but relative luxuries
like dairy products and meat. The Republic owed this advantage
in importing cheap inputs to its dominance of the Baltic trade, a
commercial advantage that was not based on competitive costs of
production at home.

Like other commercial leaders in Europe (before the dominance of capitalist Britain), the Dutch typically relied, for their
successes in international trade, on extra-economic superiority in
negotiating separate markets, rather than on competitive production in a single market: on dominance in shipping and command
of trade routes, on monopolies and trading privileges, on an
elaborate network of far-flung trading posts and settlements, on
the development of sophisticated financial practices and instruments. These 'extra-economic' advantages often relied heavily on
military force. The rising Dutch Republic devoted much of its
massive tax revenues to military expenditures, which accounted
for more of the state's expenses than did any other activity. The
Dutch engaged in some notorious military exercises for purely
commercial advantage, not only aggressive trade wars but also
such ventures as the seizure in 1602 of a Portuguese ship with an
enormously valuable cargo of unprecedented proportions, appar-

ently large enough to affect the future course of Dutch development; or the 'Amboina massacre' of English merchants in the Moluccas. When the European economy declined in the late seventeenth century, and the market for Dutch exports went with it, the link between commerce and domestic production that had marked the 'Golden Age' was drastically weakened, and the Dutch fell back on their main strength, their 'commercial sophistication', together with its extra-economic supports.

So the Dutch, like other European economies, came up against the barriers of the old commercial system in the crisis of the seventeenth century. For all their agricultural success, and for all their trade in basic commodities, they always belonged to an economy still subject to the limitations of the pre-capitalist market, not least its disproportionate dependence on luxury consumption by the wealthy few.

The pre-capitalist character of the Dutch economy is visible in other ways too. Perhaps the most important is the extent to which the Dutch ruling class depended on 'extra-economic' modes of appropriation for its wealth. One of the most striking characteristics of the Dutch social structure was the predominance of public office as a source of private wealth.[6] The decentralized organization of the Republic, with fairly autonomous provinces and cities, created a particularly fertile field for public service occupations, so the proportion of such occupations in the population of Dutch cities was very high. But more than the sheer numbers of offices, the most remarkable thing is the wealth associated with them.

Lucrative offices were an important resource for the Dutch ruling class even in the Golden Age of the Republic's commercial dominance, when wealthy landowners or financiers would often choose to use their wealth for access to such offices, even abandoning other economic activities while enriching themselves by means of large salaries associated with office, together with other advantages and privileges. In the seventeenth century, the financial and social advantages of office in city government were particularly significant, and after 1660, when the Dutch economy, together with the European economy in which it was firmly embedded, went into a decline, the value of this source of wealth became even more highly prized. In Holland, for instance, the wealth of the urban patriciate was greater than that of any other group, and the bulk of the province's most lucrative occupations were in public office of some kind.[7]

In this sense, the Dutch Republic had much in common with other non-capitalist societies that relied on 'extra-economic' exploitation or 'politically constituted property', such as the 'tax/office' state of French absolutism, in which office was a means of extracting surplus labour from peasants by means of taxation, or those wealthy city-states that acted as 'collective lordships' in relation to their adjacent countryside.

That mode of appropriation may be important in explaining the so-called 'failed transition'. While the English, driven (as we shall see in the following chapter) by distinctive market imperatives, responded to the European crisis and the decline of agricultural prices by investing to increase labour productivity and cost-effectiveness in agriculture, in the Dutch Republic, during and after the seventeenth-century crisis, there was a process of agricultural *dis*investment.[8] As agricultural prices declined, Dutch elites became even more interested in other sources of wealth, such as enhanced extra-economic commercial advantages or public office, which was more lucrative than investment in land or in other productive enterprises. While investment in technologies to enhance labour-productivity was 'not altogether lacking', it was far from being the preferred response to declining market opportunities. More attractive to the wealthy elites were 'extra-economic' strategies and investment in politically constituted property, not only office but also such attempts to revive monopoly privileges as the re-establishment of the West India Company or one company's monopoly on navigational charts.[9]

Nor did the Republic neglect the military dimension of its commercial policy. Perhaps the most striking example is the

Dutch role in England's so-called 'Glorious Revolution' of 1688. The province of Holland in particular depended on the profitability of commerce and therefore was especially affected by the incursions of French mercantilism in the late seventeenth century, its interference with Dutch ships, and its prohibitive tariffs. The only solution to this problem of commercial profitability was an extra-economic defeat of French mercantilism, and that required an alliance with England, which was possible only with a friend and ally on the English throne. The Dutch Republic therefore committed its resources to supporting William of Orange's bid for the English monarchy, in 'a risky investment to use the one resource the Republic had in abundance – money – to re-establish an international environment in which the economy could once again prosper'.[10]

The Revolution may, to the English, seem 'glorious' and largely bloodless. But from the Dutch point of view it was an invasion, with the occupation of London by Dutch troops, in full expectation of a war involving not only the English but also the French. Yet this invasion was nothing more nor less than a commercial enterprise. Not only the Dutch state but the Amsterdam stock exchange invested in this ultimate use of extra-economic power in pursuit of commercial profit.

Thereafter, although commerce continued to be the major source of the Republic's wealth, it was increasingly detached from domestic production and more dependent than ever on 'commercial sophistication'.[11] In short, there seems to be a consistent pattern of reversion to, or intensification of, pre-capitalist commercial profit-taking or even non-capitalist forms of 'extra-economic' appropriation, rentier wealth, and officeholding.

The level of commercial and technological development in the Dutch Republic set it apart from other European economies. It certainly pushed to their utmost limits the possibilities of commercialization, and it certainly made maximum use of market *opportunities*. The Republic undoubtedly relied on trade not only for its great wealth but even for its basic food requirements. In that sense, it was certainly dependent on the market. Yet the fate of the Dutch economy ultimately depended not on the successes or failures of competitive producers but on the interests of commercial profit-takers and an elite of officeholders.

The market *imperatives* that generate a specifically capitalist pattern of development seem not to have operated in the Republic as they were to do in England. Again, as in the case of Florence, it is possible to argue that this absence was as much a strength as a weakness, and that the Dutch Republic enjoyed its Golden Age not as a capitalist economy but as the last and most highly developed non-capitalist commercial society, owing its accomplishments no less to its commercial success than to its freedom from the constraints and contradictions of capitalism. But, whatever possibilities such a commercial economy may or may not have contained, once capitalism did emerge elsewhere it inevitably set the terms, for better or worse, of all economic development thereafter, not only in its birthplace but throughout the world. Especially once British capitalism assumed its industrial form, the competitive pressures it was able to impose on its rivals, either directly in commerce or by means of its military and geopolitical advantages, created new external pressures for similar developments elsewhere.

England was at the outset less advanced in commerce and technology than its Dutch rival, but its further development, both its successes and its failures, was shaped by a distinctive system of social property relations, which made both producers and appropriators irreducibly dependent on competitive production. These property relations would set in motion a relentless compulsion to compete, to produce cost-effectively, to maximize profit, to reinvest surpluses, and systematically to increase labour-productivity by improving the productive forces. With that compulsion came all the contradictions of capitalism.

5

THE AGRARIAN ORIGIN
OF CAPITALISM

The most salutary corrective to the naturalization of capitalism
and to question-begging assumptions about its origin is the
recognition that capitalism, with all its very specific drives of
accumulation and profit-maximization, was born not in the city
but in the countryside, in a very specific place, and very late in
human history. It required not a simple extension or expansion
of barter and exchange but a complete transformation in the most
basic human relations and practices, a rupture in age-old patterns
of human interaction with nature.

AGRARIAN CAPITALISM

For millennia, human beings have provided for their material
needs by working the land. And probably for nearly as long as
they have engaged in agriculture they have been divided into
classes, between those who worked the land and those who
appropriated the labour of others. That division between appropriators and producers has taken many forms, but one common
characteristic is that the direct producers have typically been
peasants. These peasant producers have generally had direct access
to the means of their own reproduction and to the land itself.
This has meant that when their surplus labour has been appropriated by exploiters, it has been done by what Marx called 'extra-
economic' means – that is, by means of direct coercion, exercised

by landlords or states employing their superior force, their privileged access to military, judicial, and political power.

In early modern France, for example, as we have seen, where production was dominated by peasant owner/occupiers, appropriation took the classic pre-capitalist form of politically constituted property, eventually giving rise not to capitalism but to the 'tax/office' structure of absolutism. Here, centralized forms of extra-economic exploitation competed with and increasingly supplanted older forms of seigneurial extraction. Office became a major means of extracting surplus labour from direct producers, in the form of tax; and the state, which became a source of great private wealth, co-opted and incorporated growing numbers of appropriators from among the old nobility as well as newer 'bourgeois' officeholders.

Here, then, is the basic difference between all pre-capitalist societies and capitalism. It has nothing to do with whether production is urban or rural and everything to do with the particular property relations between producers and appropriators, whether in industry or agriculture. Only in capitalism is the dominant mode of appropriation based on the complete dispossession of direct producers, who (unlike chattel slaves) are legally free and whose surplus labour is appropriated by purely 'economic' means. Because direct producers in a fully developed capitalism are propertyless, and because their only access to the means of production, to the requirements of their own reproduction, even to the means of their own labour, is the sale of their labour-power in exchange for a wage, capitalists can appropriate the workers' surplus labour without direct coercion.

This unique relation between producers and appropriators is, of course, mediated by the 'market'. Markets of various kinds have existed throughout recorded history and no doubt before, as people have exchanged and sold their surpluses in many different ways and for many different purposes. But the market in capitalism has a distinctive, unprecedented function. Virtually everything in capitalist society is a commodity produced for the market. And even more fundamentally, both capital and labour are utterly dependent on the market for the most basic conditions of their own reproduction. Just as workers depend on the market to sell their labour-power as a commodity, capitalists depend on it to buy labour-power, as well as the means of production, and to realize their profits by selling the goods or services produced by the workers. This market dependence gives the market an unprecedented role in capitalist societies, as not only a simple mechanism of exchange or distribution but the principal determinant and regulator of social reproduction. The emergence of the market as a determinant of social reproduction presupposed its penetration into the production of life's most basic necessity: food.

This unique system of market dependence has specific systemic requirements and compulsions shared by no other mode of production: the imperatives of competition, accumulation, and profit-maximization, and hence a constant systemic need to develop the productive forces. These imperatives, in turn, mean that capitalism can and must constantly expand in ways and degrees unlike any other social form. It can and must constantly accumulate, constantly search out new markets, constantly impose its imperatives on new territories and new spheres of life, on all human beings and the natural environment.

Once we recognize just how distinctive these social relations and processes are, how different they are from the social forms that have dominated most of human history, it becomes clear that more is required to explain the emergence of this distinctive social form than the question-begging assumption that it has always existed in embryo, just needing to be liberated from unnatural constraints.

The question of its origins can be formulated this way: given that producers were exploited by appropriators in non-capitalist ways for millennia before the advent of capitalism, and given that

markets have also existed 'time out of mind' and almost everywhere, how did it happen that producers and appropriators, and
the relations between them, came to be so market-dependent?

Now obviously the long and complex historical processes that
ultimately led to this condition of market dependence could be
traced back indefinitely. But we can make the question more
manageable by identifying the first time and place that a new
social dynamic of market dependence is clearly discernible. In the
previous chapter, we considered the nature of pre-capitalist trade
and the development of great commercial powers that flourished
by availing themselves of market opportunities without being
systematically subjected to market imperatives. Within the pre-
capitalist European economy, there was one major exception to
the general rule. England, by the sixteenth century, was developing in wholly new directions.

We can begin to see the differences by starting with the nature
of the English state and what that reveals about the relation
between political and economic power. Although there were
other relatively strong monarchical states in Europe, more or less
unified under monarchy, such as Spain and France, none was as
effectively unified as England (and the emphasis here is on
England, not other parts of the British Isles). In the eleventh
century (if not before), when the Norman ruling class established
itself on the island as a fairly cohesive military and political entity,
England already became more unified than most countries. In the
sixteenth century, England went a long way toward eliminating
the fragmentation of the state, the 'parcellized sovereignty',
inherited from feudalism. The autonomous powers held by lords,
municipal bodies, and other corporate entities in other European
states were, in England, increasingly concentrated in the central
state. This was in contrast to other European states, where
powerful monarchies continued for a long time to live uneasily
alongside other post-feudal military powers, fragmented legal
systems, and corporate privileges whose possessors insisted on
their autonomy against the centralizing power of the state – and

which continued to serve not only 'extra-economic' purposes but also as primary means of extracting surpluses from direct producers.

The distinctive political centralization of the English state had material foundations and corollaries. Already in the sixteenth century, England had an impressive network of roads and water transport that unified the nation to a degree unusual for the period. London, becoming disproportionately large in relation to other English towns and to the total population of England (and eventually the largest city in Europe), was also becoming the hub of a developing national market.

The material foundation on which this emerging national economy rested was English agriculture, which was unique in several ways. First, the English ruling class was distinctive in two related respects.[1] On the one hand, demilitarized before any other aristocracy in Europe, it was part of the increasingly centralized state, in alliance with a centralizing monarchy, without the parcellization of sovereignty characteristic of feudalism and its successor states. While the state served the ruling class as an instrument of order and protector of property, the aristocracy did not possess autonomous 'extra-economic' powers or 'politically constituted property' to the same degree as their continental counterparts.

On the other hand, there was what might be called a trade-off between the centralization of state power and the aristocracy's control of land. Land in England had for a long time been unusually concentrated, with big landlords holding an unusually large proportion, in conditions that enabled them to use their property in new ways. What they lacked in 'extra-economic' powers of surplus extraction they more than made up for with increasing 'economic' powers.

This distinctive combination had significant consequences. On the one hand, the concentration of English landholding meant that an unusually large proportion of land was worked not by peasant-proprietors but by tenants (the word 'farmer', incidentally, literally means 'tenant' – a usage suggested by phrases familiar today, such as 'farming out'). This was true even before the waves of dispossession, especially in the sixteenth and eighteenth centuries, conventionally associated with 'enclosure', and was in contrast, for example, to France, where a larger proportion of land remained, and would long continue to remain, in the hands of peasants.

On the other hand, the relatively weak extra-economic powers of landlords meant that they depended less on their ability to squeeze more rents out of their tenants by direct, coercive means than on their tenants' success in competitive production. Agrarian landlords in this arrangement had a strong incentive to encourage – and, wherever possible, to compel – their tenants to find ways of reducing costs by increasing labour-productivity.

In this respect, they were fundamentally different from rentier aristocrats, who throughout history have depended for their wealth on squeezing surpluses out of peasants by means of simple coercion, enhancing their powers of surplus extraction not by increasing the productivity of the direct producers but rather by improving their own coercive powers – military, judicial, and political.

As for the tenants, they were increasingly subject not only to direct pressures from landlords but also to market imperatives that compelled them to enhance their productivity. English tenancies took various forms, and there were many regional variations, but a growing number were subject to economic rents – rents fixed not by some legal or customary standard but by market conditions. There was, in effect, a market in leases. Tenants were obliged to compete not only in a market for consumers but also in a market for access to land.

The effect of this system of property relations was that many agricultural producers (including prosperous 'yeomen') became market-dependent in their access to land itself, to the means of production. Increasingly, as more land came under this economic regime, advantage in access to the land itself would go to those who could produce competitively and pay good rents by increasing their own productivity. This meant that success would breed success, and competitive farmers would have increasing access to even more land, while others lost access altogether.

This market-mediated relation between landlords and peasants is visible in the attitude to rents that was emerging by the sixteenth century. In a system of 'competitive rents', in which landlords, wherever possible, would effectively lease land to the highest bidder, at whatever rent the market would bear, they – and their surveyors – became increasingly conscious of the difference between the fixed rents paid by customary tenants and an economic rent determined by the market.[2] We can watch the development of a new mentality by observing the landlord's surveyor as he computes the rental value of land on the basis of some more or less abstract principle of market value, and measures it explicitly against the actual rents being paid by customary tenants. Here, in the careful estimates of these surveyors, who talk about 'the annual value beyond rent' or 'value above the oulde [sic] rent', and in their calculation of what they consider to be the unearned increment that goes to the copyhold tenant paying a customary rent below the value of land determined by competitive market conditions, we have the rudiments of later, more sophisticated theories of value and capitalist ground rent. These conceptions of value are based on the very concrete experience of landlords at a critical moment in the development of the competitive system of agrarian capitalism.

The development of these economic rents illustrates the difference between the market as opportunity and the market as imperative. It also exposes the deficiencies in accounts of capitalist development based on the conventional assumptions. The ways in which those assumptions have determined perceptions of the evidence is nicely illustrated in an important article from the transition debate on the structural role of towns in feudalism. John Merrington suggests that although the transformation of feudal surplus labour into monetary rents did not in itself alter the fundamental nature of feudal relations, it did have one important consequence: by helping to fix surplus labour to a constant magnitude it 'stimulated the growth of independent commodity production'.[3]

But this proposition seems to be based less on empirical evidence than on the market-as-opportunity model, with its assumption that petty producers would choose to act like capitalists if only given the chance. The effects of monetary rents varied widely according to the property relations between the peasants who produced those rents and the landlords who appropriated them. Where the extra-economic powers of feudal lords remained strong, peasants could be subjected to the same coercive pressures as before from landlords seeking to squeeze more surplus labour out of them, even if now it took the form of monetary rents instead of labour services. Where, as in France, the peasantry's hold on property was strong enough to resist such increasing pressures from landlords, rents were often fixed at a nominal rate.

Surely it is precisely in a case like this, with peasants enjoying secure property rights and subject not only to fixed but also to modest rents, that we might, on the basis of Merrington's assumptions, expect to find a stimulus to commodity production that might eventually give rise to capitalism. But the effect was just the opposite. The evidence outlined by Brenner suggests that it was not fixed rents of this kind that stimulated the growth of commodity production. On the contrary, it was unfixed, variable rents responsive to market imperatives that in England stimulated the development of commodity production, the improvement of productivity, and self-sustaining economic development. In France, precisely because peasants typically enjoyed possession of land at fixed and nominal rents, no such stimulus existed. It was, in other words, not the *opportunities* afforded by the market but rather its *imperatives* that drove petty commodity producers to accumulate.

By the early modern period, even many customary leases in

England had effectively become economic leases of this kind. But even those tenants who enjoyed some kind of customary tenure that gave them more security, but who might still be obliged to sell their produce in the same markets, could go under in conditions where competitive standards of productivity were being set by farmers responding more directly and urgently to the pressures of the market. The same would increasingly be true even of landowners working their own land. In this competitive environment, productive farmers prospered and their holdings were likely to grow, while less competitive producers went to the wall and joined the propertyless classes.

So, as competitive market forces established themselves, less productive farmers lost their property. Market forces were, no doubt, assisted by direct coercive intervention to evict tenants or to extinguish their customary rights. Perhaps some historians have exaggerated the decline of the English peasantry, which may have taken much longer to disappear completely than some accounts suggest. But there can be little doubt that in comparison with other European peasantries, the English variety was a rare and endangered species, and market imperatives certainly accelerated the polarization of English rural society into larger landowners and a growing propertyless multitude. The famous triad of landlord, capitalist tenant, and wage labourer was the result, and with the growth of wage labour the pressures to improve labour-productivity also increased. The same process created a highly productive agriculture capable of sustaining a large population not engaged in agricultural production, but also an increasing propertyless mass that would constitute both a large wage-labour force and a domestic market for cheap consumer goods – a type of market with no historical precedent. This is the background to the formation of English industrial capitalism.

The contrast with France is illuminating. The crisis of French feudalism was resolved by a different kind of state formation. Here, the aristocracy long retained its hold on politically consti-tuted property, but when feudalism was replaced by absolutism, politically constituted property was not replaced by purely economic exploitation or capitalist production. Instead, the French ruling class gained new extra-economic powers as the absolutist state created a vast apparatus of office by means of which a section of the propertied class could appropriate the surplus labour of peasants in the form of tax. Even then, at the height of absolutism, France remained a confusing welter of competing jurisdictions, as nobility and municipal authorities clung to the remnants of their autonomous feudal powers, the residues of feudal 'parcellized sovereignty'. These residual powers and privileges, even when they ceased to have much political force, were jealously preserved – and even revived or reinvented – as economic resources.

The divergence between property relations in France and those in England is nicely encapsulated in the contrast between the mind-set of the late sixteenth- or early seventeenth-century English land surveyor we encountered before and that of his French counterpart, then and long thereafter. While the English were preoccupied with market valuations and competitive rents, at a time when French peasants were consolidating rights of inheritance and French lords had little benefit from rents, the French surveyor was obsessively combing the records for any sign of seigneurial rights and peasant obligations that could be revived – or even invented. So while the English went in search of 'real' market values, the French were using the most up-to-date and scientific methods to chart a revival of feudalism.[4]

In these conditions, where the preferred economic strategy for ruling classes was still to squeeze the peasants by extra-economic means rather than to encourage competitive production and 'improvement', there was no impetus to capitalist development comparable to England's – until England itself succeeded in imposing its competitive pressures on an international economy. If anything, the effect of the French system of social property relations 'was to prove disastrous to economic development'. In its efforts to preserve its tax-producing base, the absolutist state strengthened old forms of peasant possession, and the new system of surplus extraction 'was oriented even more single-mindedly to conspicuous consumption and war'.[5] This system was more effective than the old in squeezing surplus out of the direct producers, which meant not only that there was little incentive for the appropriators to encourage labour productivity and the development of productive forces but also that it was even more of a drain on the productive forces of the peasantry.

It is worth noting, too, that while the integrated national market – which Polanyi described as the first kind of market to operate on competitive principles – developed in England quite early, France had to await the Napoleonic era to remove internal barriers to trade. The important point is that the development of a competitive national market was a corollary, not a cause, of capitalism and market society. The evolution of a unified, competitive national market reflected changes in the mode of exploitation and the nature of the state.

So, for example, in France, the persistence of politically constituted property, or 'extra-economic' forms of exploitation, meant that neither the state nor the economy was truly integrated. Powers of exploitation that were political and economic at the same time, in the form of state office as well as the remnants of old aristocratic and municipal jurisdictions, tended to fragment both state and economy even under absolutism. In England, there was a clearer separation between the political, coercive powers of the state and the exploitative powers of propertied classes that derived their wealth from purely 'economic' forms of exploitation. The private economic powers of the ruling class did not detract from the political unity of the state, and there was both a truly centralized state and an integrated national economy.

THE RISE OF CAPITALIST PROPERTY
AND THE ETHIC OF 'IMPROVEMENT'

English agriculture, then, was already in the sixteenth century marked by a unique combination of conditions, at least in certain regions, that would gradually set the economic direction of the whole economy. The result was a highly productive agrarian sector, in which landlords and tenants alike became preoccupied with what they called 'improvement', the enhancement of the land's productivity for profit.

It is worth dwelling for a moment on this concept of improvement, because it tells us a great deal about English agriculture and the development of capitalism. The word 'improve' itself, in its original meaning, did not mean just 'make better' in a general sense but literally meant to do something for monetary profit, especially to cultivate land for profit (based on the old French for *into*, *en*, and *profit*, *pros* – or its oblique case, *preu*). By the seventeenth century, the word 'improver' was firmly fixed in the language to refer to someone who rendered land productive and profitable, especially by enclosing it or reclaiming waste. Agricultural improvement was by then a well-established practice, and in the eighteenth century, in the golden age of agrarian capitalism, 'improvement' in word and deed came truly into its own.

The word was at the same time acquiring a more general meaning in the sense that we know it today. (We might like to think about the implications of a culture in which the word for 'making better' is rooted in the word for monetary profit.) Even in its association with agriculture, it eventually lost some of its old specificity – so that, for example, some radical thinkers in the nineteenth century might embrace improvement in the sense of scientific farming, without its connotation of commercial profit. But in the early modern period, productivity and profit were inextricably connected in the concept of improvement, and it nicely sums up the ideology of a rising agrarian capitalism.

In the seventeenth century a whole new body of literature emerged, spelling out in unprecedented detail the techniques and benefits of improvement. Improvement was also a major preoccupation of the Royal Society, which brought together some of England's most prominent scientists (Isaac Newton and Robert Boyle were both members) with some of the more forward-looking members of England's ruling classes – like the first Earl of Shaftesbury, mentor of the philosopher John Locke, and Locke himself, both of whom were keenly interested in agricultural improvement.

Improvement did not, in the first instance, depend on significant technological innovations – although new equipment was used, like the wheel-plough. In general, it was more a matter of new developments in farming techniques or even just refinements and elaborations of old ones: 'convertible' or 'up and down' husbandry, alternating tillage and pasture; crop rotation; drainage of marsh and ploughlands; and so on.

But improvement meant something more than new or better methods and techniques of farming. Improvement meant, even more fundamentally, new forms and conceptions of property. 'Improved' farming, for the enterprising landlord and his prosperous capitalist tenant, ideally though not necessarily meant enlarged and concentrated landholdings. It certainly meant the elimination of old customs and practices that interfered with the most productive use of land.

Peasants have since time immemorial employed various means of regulating land use in the interests of the village community. They have restricted certain practices and granted certain rights, not in order to enhance the wealth of landlords or states but in order to preserve the peasant community itself, perhaps to conserve the land or to distribute its fruits more equitably, and often to provide for the community's less fortunate members. Even private ownership of property has been typically conditioned by such customary practices, giving non-owners certain use rights to property owned by someone else. In England, there were many such practices and customs. There existed common lands, on which members of the community might have grazing rights or the right to collect firewood, and there were various other kinds of use rights on private land, such as the right to collect the leavings of the harvest during specified periods of the year.

From the standpoint of improving landlords and capitalist

farmers, land had to be liberated from any such obstruction to their productive and profitable use of property. Between the sixteenth and eighteenth centuries, there was growing pressure to extinguish customary rights that interfered with capitalist accumulation. This could mean various things: disputing communal rights to common lands by claiming exclusive private ownership; eliminating various use rights on private land; or challenging the customary tenures that gave many smallholders rights of possession without unambiguous legal title. In all these cases, traditional conceptions of property had to be replaced by new, capitalist conceptions of property – not only as 'private' but as *exclusive*. Other individuals and the community had to be excluded by eliminating village regulation and restrictions on land use (something that did not, for example, happen in France in anything like the same ways and degrees), especially by extinguishing customary use rights.[6]

ENCLOSURE

This brings us to the most famous redefinition of property rights: enclosure. Enclosure is often thought of as simply the fencing in of common land, or of the 'open fields' that characterized certain parts of the English countryside. But enclosure meant not simply a physical fencing of land but the extinction of common and customary use rights on which many people depended for their livelihood.

Early enclosures were sometimes undertaken by, or with the agreement of, smaller farmers and not always to their detriment. But the first major wave of socially disruptive enclosure occurred in the sixteenth century, when larger landowners sought to drive commoners off lands that could be profitably put to use as pasture for increasingly lucrative sheep farming. Contemporary commentators held enclosure, more than any other single factor, responsible for the growing plague of vagabonds, those dispossessed 'masterless men' who wandered the countryside and threatened social order.[7] The most famous of these commentators, Thomas More, though himself an encloser, described the practice as 'sheep devouring men'. These social critics, like many historians after them, may have overestimated the effects of enclosure at the expense of other factors leading to the transformation of English property relations. But it remains the most vivid expression of the relentless process that was changing not only the English country-side but also the world: the birth of capitalism.

Enclosure continued to be a major source of conflict in early modern England, whether for sheep or increasingly profitable arable farming. Enclosure riots punctuated the sixteenth and seventeenth centuries, and enclosure surfaced as a major grievance in the English Civil War. In its earlier phases, the practice was to some degree resisted by the monarchical state, if only because of the threat to public order. But once the landed classes had succeeded in shaping the state to their own changing require-ments – a success more or less finally consolidated in 1688, in the so-called 'Glorious Revolution' – there was no further state interference, and a new kind of enclosure movement emerged in the eighteenth century, the so-called 'Parliamentary enclosures'. In this kind of enclosure, the extinction of troublesome property rights that interfered with some landlord's powers of accumula-tion took place by acts of Parliament. Nothing more neatly testifies to the triumph of agrarian capitalism.

LOCKE'S THEORY OF PROPERTY

The pressures to transform the nature of property manifested themselves in various ways, in theory and in practice. They surfaced in court cases, in conflicts over specific property rights, over some piece of common land or some private land to which different people had overlapping use rights. In such cases, custom-ary practices and claims often directly confronted the principles of 'improvement' – and judges often recognized reasons of improvement as legitimate claims against customary rights that had been in place as long as anyone could remember.[8] New conceptions of property were also being theorized more systematically, most famously in Chapter 5 of John Locke's *Second Treatise of Government*, written in the late seventeenth century.[9] It is worth looking more closely at his argument, because there is no other work more emblematic of a rising agrarian capitalism.

Locke begins with the proposition that God 'hath given the world to men in common' (II.26), but he goes on to show how, nevertheless, individuals came to have property in particular things. In fact, he writes, such private, individual property is a God-given natural right. Men (and in his argument, it is always men) own their own persons, and the labour that they do with their hands and bodies is therefore their property too. So, he argues, a natural right of property is established when a man 'mixes his labour' with something, when, that is, by means of his labour he removes it from its natural state or changes its natural condition.

Locke was certainly not the first thinker to propose that unoccupied land could be claimed by those who would render it fruitful, but, as he developed his labour theory of property, he introduced some enormously significant innovations. We shall consider some of their implications more closely in Chapter 7, in connection with the ideology of imperialism. For now, the central point is that Locke's whole argument on property turns on the notion of 'improvement'.

The theme running throughout his discussion is that the earth is there to be made productive and profitable, and that this is why private property, which emanates from labour, trumps common possession. Locke repeatedly insists that most of the value inherent in land comes not from nature but from labour and improvement: ''tis *labour* indeed that *puts the difference of value* on everything' (II.40). He even offers specific calculations of value contributed by labour as against nature. He suggests, for example, 'it will be but a very modest Computation to say, that of the *Products* of the Earth useful to the Life of Man, 9/10 are the *effects of labour*,' and then immediately corrects himself: it would be more accurate to say that 99/100 should be attributed to labour rather than to nature (II.40).

Locke also makes it clear that the value he has in mind is not simply *use* value but *exchange* value. Money and commerce are the motivation for improvement; and an acre of land in unimproved America, which may be as naturally fertile as an acre in England, is not worth 1/1000 of the English acre, if we calculate 'all the Profit an *Indian* received from it were it valued and sold here' (II.43). Locke's point, which not coincidentally drips with colonialist contempt, is that unimproved land is *waste*, so that any man who takes it out of common ownership and appropriates it to himself – he who removes land from the common and encloses it – in order to improve it has *given* something to humanity, not taken it away.

There is, of course, something attractive about Locke's idea that labour is the source of value and the basis of property, but it soon becomes clear that there is something odd about it too. For one thing, it turns out that there is no direct correspondence between labour and property, because one man can appropriate the labour of another. He can acquire a right of property in something by 'mixing' with it not his own labour but the labour of someone else whom he employs. It appears that the issue for Locke has less to do with the activity of labour as such than with its profitable use. In calculating the value of the acre in America, for instance, he talks not about the Indian's expenditure of effort, labour, but about the Indian's failure to realize a profit. The issue, in other words, is not the labour of a human being but the *productivity of property*, its exchange value and its application to commercial profit.

This emphasis on the creation of exchange value as the basis of property is a critical move in the theorization of capitalist property. Locke certainly was not the first to claim that people have a right to take possession of unoccupied and unused land, if they are able and willing to render it fruitful. His idea that property derives from labour is not so distant from that traditional notion. What makes his theory truly distinctive is the association of 'labour' with the creation of exchange value, and the derivation of property from the creation of exchange value. This had implications not only for domestic property relations but also, as we shall see, for the justification of colonial expropriation. It could be used to defend the enclosure of 'unprofitable' land at home, as well as territory in the colonies that was not being put to commercially profitable use by indigenous populations.

In a famous and much debated passage, Locke writes that 'the Grass my Horse has bit; the Turfs my Servant has cut; and the Ore I have digg'd in any place where I have a right to them in common with others, become my *Property* . . .' (II.28). Much ink has been spilled on this passage and what it tells us about, for example, Locke's views on wage labour (the labour of the servant who cuts the turfs). But what is truly striking about the passage is that Locke treats 'the Turfs my Servant has cut' as equivalent to 'the Ore I have digg'd'. This means not only that I, the master, have appropriated the labour of my servant, but also that this appropriation is in principle no different from the servant's labouring activity itself. My own digging is, for all intents and purposes, the same as my appropriating the fruits of my servant's cutting. But Locke is not interested in simply *passive* appropriation. The point is rather that the landlord who puts his land to productive use, who improves it, even if it is by means of someone else's labour, is being *industrious*, no less – and perhaps more – than the labouring servant.

This is a point worth dwelling on. One way of understanding what Locke is driving at is to consider common usage today. When the financial pages of the daily newspaper speak of 'producers', they do not normally mean *workers*. In fact, they are likely to talk about conflicts, for example, between automobile 'producers' and auto workers or their unions. The employers of labour, in other words, are being credited with 'production'. We have become so accustomed to this usage that we fail to see its implications, but it is important to keep in mind that certain very specific historical conditions were required to make it possible.

Traditional ruling classes in a pre-capitalist society, passively appropriating rents from dependent peasants, would never think of themselves as 'producers'. The kind of appropriation that can be called 'productive' is distinctively capitalist. It implies that property is used *actively*, not for conspicuous consumption but for investment and increasing profit. Wealth is acquired not simply by using coercive force to extract more surplus labour from direct producers, in the manner of rentier aristocrats, nor by buying cheap and selling dear like pre-capitalist merchants, but by increasing labour-productivity (output per unit of work).

By conflating labour with the production of profit, Locke becomes perhaps the first thinker to construct a systematic theory of property based on something like these capitalist principles. He is certainly not a theorist of a mature, industrial capitalism. But his view of property, with its emphasis on productivity and exchange value created in production, already sets him apart from his predecessors. His idea that value is actively created in production is already vastly different from traditional views that focus simply on the process of exchange, the 'sphere of circulation'. Only William Petty, often called the founder of political economy, had suggested anything like a 'labour theory of value' in the seventeenth century, and that too in the context of agrarian capitalism – a theory he tested as a colonial agent in Ireland, where he served as Cromwell's Surveyor General, just as Locke and his mentor the first Earl of Shaftesbury looked upon the American colonies as a laboratory of improvement.[10]

Locke in his economic works is critical of those landed aristocrats who sit back and collect rents without improving their land, and he is equally critical of merchants who simply act as middlemen, buying cheap in one market and selling at a higher price in another, or hoarding goods to raise their price, or cornering a market to increase the profits of sale. Both types of proprietor are, in his view, parasitic. Yet his attack on proprietors of this kind should not be misread as a defence of working people against the dominant classes. He certainly has good things to say about industrious artisans and tradesmen, but his ideal seems to be the great improving landlord, whom he regards as the ultimate source of wealth in the community, what he calls, significantly, the 'first producer' – a man like Shaftesbury, capitalist landlord and investor in colonial trade, a man who is not only 'industrious' but whose vast property contributes greatly to the wealth of the community.

Locke's view of property is very well suited to the conditions of England in the early days of agrarian capitalism. It clearly reflects a condition in which highly concentrated landownership and large holdings were associated with a highly productive agriculture (again, productive in the sense not just of total output but also of output per unit of work). His language of improvement echoes the scientific literature devoted to the techniques of agriculture that flourished uniquely in England at this time – especially emanating from the Royal Society and the groups of learned men with whom Locke and Shaftesbury were closely connected. More particularly, his constant references to common land as *waste* and his praise for the removal of land from the common, and indeed for enclosure, had very powerful resonances in that time and place.

We need to be reminded that the definition of property was in Locke's day not just a philosophical issue but a very immediate practical one. As we have seen, a new, capitalist definition of property was in the process of establishing itself, challenging traditional forms not just in theory but also in practice. The idea of overlapping use rights to the same piece of land was giving way in England to *exclusive* ownership. From the sixteenth to the eighteenth century, there were constant disputes over common and customary rights. Increasingly, the principle of improvement for profitable exchange was taking precedence over other principles and other claims to property, whether those claims were based on custom or on some fundamental right of subsistence.

Enhancing productivity itself became a reason for excluding other rights.

What better argument than Locke's could be found to support the landlord seeking to extinguish the customary rights of commoners, to exclude them from common land, and to turn common land into exclusive private property by means of enclosure? What better argument than that enclosure, exclusion, and improvement enhanced the wealth of the community and added more to the 'common stock' than it subtracted? And indeed, there were in the seventeenth century already examples of legal decisions in conflicts over land where judges invoked principles very much like those outlined by Locke, in order to give exclusive property precedence over common and customary rights. In the eighteenth century, when enclosure would accelerate rapidly with the active involvement of Parliament, reasons of 'improvement' would be cited systematically as the basis of title to property and as grounds for extinguishing traditional rights.

This is not the only way in which Locke's theory of property supported the interests of landlords like Shaftesbury. Against the background of his emphatic pronouncement that all men were free and equal in the state of nature, he nevertheless, like others before him, justified slavery. More particularly, as we shall see in Chapter 7, his views on improvement could easily be mobilized to justify colonial expansion and the expropriation of indigenous peoples, as his remark on the American Indian makes painfully obvious. If the unimproved lands of the Americas represented nothing but 'waste', it was a divinely ordained duty for Europeans to enclose and improve them, just as 'industrious' and 'rational' men had done in the original state of nature. 'In the beginning all the World was *America*' (II.49), with no money, no commerce, no improvement. If the world – or some of it – had been removed from that natural state at the behest of God, anything that remained in such a primitive condition must surely go the same way.

CLASS STRUGGLE AND
BOURGEOIS REVOLUTION

It should be clear at this point that the development of distinctive property forms in English agriculture entailed new forms of class struggle. Here again, we can highlight the specificity of agrarian capitalism by contrasting the English situation to the French. The differences in property forms and modes of exploitation that, as we have seen, characterized these two major European powers were reflected in different issues and terrains of class struggle, and different relations between class and state.

In France, extra-economic modes of surplus extraction or politically constituted property, whether in the form of state office or the various powers and privileges attached to noble status (such as certain exemptions from taxes), set the terms of class struggle. The state, for instance, served as a source of income for a substantial segment of the dominant classes. At the same time, the state, as a form of politically constituted property, competed with landed classes for the same peasant-produced surpluses. So parts of the aristocracy might struggle against the efforts of the monarchy to suppress their autonomous powers and appropriate them to a centralized absolutist state, while others held or sought to acquire property in that very state. A bourgeois might oppose the excessive burden of taxation borne by the unprivileged Third Estate and the exemptions enjoyed by the privileged estates, the nobility and the church, while at the same time he might seek state office (which could be bought) as a means of appropriating surplus labour through taxation. Peasants were, of course, the primary source of that surplus labour, which meant that, as the state and its apparatus of offices grew and peasants were subject to an ever-increasing burden of taxation, the peasantry had to be preserved by the monarchy from destruction by rent-hungry landlords in order to be squeezed by a tax-hungry state.

Appropriating classes, then, had a material interest in preserving or obtaining access to politically constituted property, whether in the form of privilege or directly in state office. This would prove a major issue in the Revolution of 1789, when aristocratic privilege was challenged by the Third Estate, and when the bourgeoisie in particular reacted against the threat to close their access to state office.[11] For producing classes, and peasants in particular, the single largest class issue throughout the *ancien régime* was undoubtedly the burden of taxation, and popular resistance was likely to focus above all on exploitation by the state in the form of steeply rising taxes.

The picture was very different in early modern England. There, politically constituted property was not a major issue. The landed class, in its growing reliance on purely economic forms of exploitation, never relied so much on the state as a direct material resource, and royal taxation never played the same role for the English propertied classes that it did for the French. While English landlords relied on the state to enforce their class interests – and would come into conflict with it when their property, or the powers of Parliament as a committee of propertyholders, were challenged by the monarchy – their direct material interests lay not in acquiring a piece of the state so much as in enhancing their *economic* powers of appropriation, the powers rooted directly in their control of land and its productive uses. While the French aristocrat might be preoccupied with retaining his access to high office or his tax exemptions and various noble privileges, the right of enclosure might figure more prominently on the class agenda of the English landlord.

For subordinate classes in England, this meant that conflicts over property rights, over the very meaning of property, loomed larger than struggles against extra-economic exploitation. So, for instance, resistance to enclosure, or the protection of customary use rights, would, for the English commoner, occupy the prominent position in struggles against exploitation that resistance to taxation did for the French peasant. While French peasants struggled against taxation, the English peasant revolts of the sixteenth century, for instance, were directed against landlords who were raising fines and rents by seeking to impose the norms of the market.

This also raises some important questions about the role of class struggle in the development of capitalism. What, for instance, can we say now about the argument that class struggle by peasants against landlords promoted capitalism in England by throwing off the shackles of feudalism and liberating commodity production? While the configuration of class relations was too complex to be reduced to any simple formula, if we want to sum up in a single sentence the ways in which class struggle between landlords and peasants 'liberated' capitalism, it might be closer to the truth to say that capitalism was advanced by the assertion of the landlords' powers against the peasants' claims to customary rights.

To say this is also, of course, to cast doubt on the characterization of the seventeenth-century English Revolution as a 'bourgeois revolution' and, indeed, on the whole concept of 'bourgeois revolution'. Calling this revolution 'bourgeois' requires a definition so vague and general as to be vacuous. At the very least, it begs the question by conflating 'bourgeois' and 'capitalist'. The proposition that capitalism was brought about by bourgeois revolutions becomes little more than a tautology.

To be sure, the concept has undergone many redefinitions among Marxist historians, and it no longer implies a simple class war between feudal aristocrats and capitalist bourgeois, from which the rising bourgeoisie emerges triumphant to liberate a fettered capitalism. Instead, it seems to apply to any revolutionary upheaval that, in one way or another, sooner or later, advances the rise of capitalism, by changing property forms or the nature of the state, irrespective of the class forces involved. This has the virtue of emphasizing the radical transformations required to bring about capitalism, but such an all-embracing notion obscures as much as it reveals.

The concept of 'bourgeois revolution' is confusing for several reasons. Was a revolution necessary to bring about capitalism, or simply to facilitate the development of an already existing capitalism? Was it a cause or an effect of capitalism? Although much has been claimed for bourgeois revolution as the critical moment in the transition to capitalism, no conception of bourgeois revolution exists in which the revolution explains the emergence of capitalism or capitalists. All of them must assume the prior existence of fairly well-developed capitalist formations, which themselves create revolutionary pressures as they find their own development thwarted by pre-capitalist classes and institutions. The bourgeois revolution, then, seems to be more effect than cause, and we are still without an explanation of the social transformations that brought capitalism into being.

Nevertheless, if capitalism pre-exists the revolution, it can, of course, still be argued that bourgeois revolution is an *effect* of capitalist relations and a factor in their further development. It is reasonable enough to argue that no development of capitalism has ever occurred without some kind of violent historic rupture. Yet the concept of bourgeois revolution is called upon to explain both cases (like England) in which revolution occurs precisely because capitalist social property relations are already well developed and an already dominant capitalist class must sweep away obstructions in the state, while subduing subordinate classes that stand in its way; and also cases (like France) in which, on the contrary, revolution occurs because aspiring capitalists (or a bourgeoisie we must assume to consist of aspiring capitalists) must defeat a dominant non-capitalist class. Contrasting these two cases, we may be forced to conclude (as suggested in Chapter 3) that revolutions can be 'bourgeois' without being capitalist and capitalist without being bourgeois.

In England, if the Revolution advanced the development of capitalism, it was largely by consolidating the position of a landed class, which was already dominant not only in society but also in the state. The revolution was not a class struggle that gave victory to a capitalist bourgeoisie against a ruling class thwarting its progress. The class struggle that certainly did take place within the Revolution was between that ruling class and subordinate popular forces, whose class interests had as much to do with opposing as promoting the progress of those capitalist landlords or their bourgeois collaborators.

This is not, again, to dismiss the role of 'middling' farmers, or the English yeoman, in the development of capitalism. These farmers, as capitalist tenants, were the backbone of the agrarian triad. But it is one thing to acknowledge this, and quite another, for instance, to treat popular-radical forces in the seventeenth-century English Revolution as simply the agents of capitalist progress. It is surely misleading to treat popular struggles as the major force in advancing the development of capitalism, empha-sizing them at the expense of more subversive and democratic popular struggles that *challenged* property forms conducive to capitalist development. These popular forces may have lost the battle against capitalist landlords, but they left a tremendous legacy of radical ideas quite distinct from the 'progressive' impulses of capitalism, a legacy that is still alive today in various democratic and anti-capitalist movements.[12]

The French Revolution of 1789 fits the description of a 'bourgeois revolution' far better than the English one – if what we are looking for is a major struggle between bourgeoisie and aristocracy. But, as we have seen, there are some very large questions about what the struggle in France had to do with capitalism.

It must be said, first, that the bourgeoisie and aristocracy had to a great extent converged in their economic positions and sources of income. Nevertheless, a conflict between them did emerge, especially over access to the lucrative resource of state office. In that sense, the revolution did become 'bourgeois', though the pressures that brought it about had less to do with capitalism than with the tensions of absolutism and state-centralization. In any case, the revolutionary bourgeoisie was not, in the main, a capitalist class even in its aspirations. The professionals and officeholders at the heart of the 'bourgeois revolution' were more interested in civil equality among the Estates and the elimination of privilege, or, to put it another way, they were more concerned with *non*-capitalist, 'extra-economic', appropriation – in particular, taxation and access to office.

As for the peasants, however much they opposed the vestiges of feudalism that the nobility always sought to impose on them, or the absolutist state that burdened them with taxation, they were certainly not capitalists, even in embryo. Nor is it easy to imagine that, if the most radical popular forces that drove the bourgeoisie beyond its own revolutionary aspirations had finally triumphed, capitalism would have been brought any closer.

The immediate effects of the Revolution if anything entrenched rather than removed pre-capitalist forms – not only consolidating the peasantry but also encouraging the growth of the state and state office as the preferred bourgeois career. It is, nonetheless, possible to make a case that the long-term effect was to facilitate the development of capitalism, for instance by unifying the state and removing internal barriers to trade. But it remains at least an open question whether that process would have advanced the development of capitalism if France had not been subject to external pressures emanating from a capitalist Britain. At any rate, given the class interests of the revolutionary bourgeoisie, it is tempting to say that the French bourgeoise was revolutionary precisely because, and to the extent that, it was *not* capitalist.

The English Revolution, by contrast, was certainly not a conflict between bourgeoisie and aristocracy. But by enhancing the power of the propertied classes in Parliament and by advancing the interests of larger against smaller landowners, and 'improvement' against the customary rights of subordinate classes, it had more to do, and more directly, with the promotion of capitalism and the capitalist definition of property than did the Revolution in France.

PART III

Agrarian Capitalism
and Beyond

6

AGRARIAN CAPITALISM AND BEYOND

In England, where wealth still derived predominantly from agricultural production, all major economic actors in the agrarian sector – both direct producers and the appropriators of their surpluses – were, from the sixteenth century, increasingly dependent on what amounted to capitalist practices: the maximization of exchange value by means of cost-cutting and improving productivity, through specialization, accumulation, reinvestment of surpluses, and innovation.

This mode of providing for the basic material needs of English society brought with it a whole new dynamic of self-sustaining development, a process of accumulation and expansion very different from the age-old 'Malthusian' cycles that dominated material life in other societies. It was also accompanied by the typical capitalist processes of expropriation and the creation of a propertyless mass. It is in this sense that the new historical dynamic allows us to speak of 'agrarian capitalism' in early modern England, a social form with distinctive 'laws of motion' that would eventually give rise to capitalism in its mature, industrial form.

THE GOLDEN AGE OF AGRARIAN CAPITALISM

Looking back at earlier centuries, it is easy to romanticize the English countryside. From the vantage point of today's agricultural crisis in Britain, against the background of 'mad cow disease' and the foot-and-mouth disaster in 2001, which exposed the horrors and dangers of intensive farming, the stranglehold on food distribution exerted by the massive supermarket chains, and the consequences of 'globalization', it is very hard to recognize the continuities between the British agricultural industry today and the landscape of the English rural idyll.

Many commentators during the recent crisis seemed to be convinced that the trends culminating in these disasters of intensive capitalist agriculture emerged only in the wake of World War II, when governments – later aided and abetted by the European Common Agricultural Policy – encouraged intensive production in order to guarantee cheap and plentiful food. Even critics on the left laid the blame for agricultural disaster on the stubborn attachment of the British public to cheap food.

It seems odd that reasonable people who have little trouble accepting that there are certain basic human needs – such as health care or education – that are best met by public services and not by profit-making enterprises regard it as unreasonable to demand cheap access to the most irreducible necessity, food. This attitude is especially puzzling because food in Britain is not particularly cheap, and the proceeds of lower production costs clearly shore up the profits of the food industry at least as much as they reduce the prices to consumers. But what is most remarkable is the conviction that today's capitalist agriculture marks a revolutionary break from the past.

At the height of the foot-and-mouth crisis in Britain, a national newspaper quoted an angry Belgian veterinary inspector complaining, 'The British value their land only to extract profit from it.' This remark, which seemed to set Britain apart from its European neighbours, may have been a nostalgic lament for a peasant culture that is hardly more real on the Continent today than it is in Britain. But the fact remains that Britain has long been in a class by itself as the homeland of agrarian capitalism.

The continuities between the old and the new agriculture are disguised by the paradoxes of agrarian capitalism. The landscape at the heart of the rural idyll is not the product of a peasant society or a countryside of independent family farms. It is largely the creation of agrarian capitalism in its 'golden age'. Although it was centuries in the making, and though the marks of other times and other ways of life have never been completely erased, the landscape that figures most prominently in the mythology of 'England's green and pleasant land' probably owes more to the eighteenth century than any other, 'the age of the territorial aristocracy' and the era of 'improvement' at its height.[1]

The seemingly idyllic landscape of rural England has inscribed within it the history of capitalist property and class relations. Both peasants and landlords underwent a transformation, which changed the landscape too. On one side is the process of dispossession and enclosure, which, among other things, made rural poverty less visible. Poor peasants of the type that have shaped the countryside in other agricultural societies, with their marginal plots and impoverished dwellings, were replaced by two distinct agrarian classes: more prosperous capitalist tenants, with their solid, even picturesque farmhouses, and landless labourers, whose only mark on the landscape was a system of rights-of-way across fields giving them access to their places of work – their gift to ramblers today. Even whole villages disappeared in this process of rural transformation. On the other side are country houses, parks, and landscape gardens. The remains of a classic military aristocrary had long been replaced by the comforts and ornaments of the country gentleman, the 'territorial aristocrat' living on the rents of capitalist tenants, who truly came into his own in the eighteenth century.

The Parliamentary enclosures of the eighteenth century sum up the paradoxes nicely. They testify to the unchallenged victory of the landed class at the heart of agrarian capitalism, its control of the land, its possession of the state, and its triumph over subordinate classes that had challenged its ascendancy in the revolution of the seventeenth century. Yet the visual legacy of that class victory, bringing to fruition a process begun in earlier centuries, has come to represent the idyll of old England.

The same paradox is contained in the notion of 'improvement'. In the eighteenth century, this serviceable concept combined profit with beauty in the interests of the landed aristocracy. To 'improve' the land meant not only to consolidate and enclose it for the purpose of increasing productivity and profit but also to beautify the landlord's estate, even if that meant erasing whole villages to remove an obstruction to the master's view and replace them with gardens and parks.

This was still a period in which productive and profitable farming methods were, by today's standards, largely 'organic', depending more on efficient land-use and farming techniques than on industrial machinery and chemicals. So the effects on the land were not so obviously damaging, however much the lives of human beings were affected by dispossession and competitive pressures. But the economic logic being played out today in the destruction of the countryside was already at work and had been for some time, at least since the sixteenth and seventeenth centuries.

It was at work when English landlords even in the sixteenth century, in parts of the country, were looking to enhance the commercial profits of their tenants, in order to extract maximum rents. It was at work when the landlord's surveyor was calculating the difference between the fixed customary rents many tenants were paying and the higher rents the landlord could obtain in an open market for leases.

The same logic was at work in the seventeenth-century explosion of 'improvement' literature; and, in the following century, the calculations that drove the Parliamentary enclosures in the interests of 'improvement' were not so very different from today's economic arithmetic. The pressures for intensified production and profitability have been infinitely aggravated by the growth of supermarket chains and globalization, and the technical possibilities of industrialized agriculture have increased beyond measure. But at the root of the problem now, as it was then, is the logic of capitalist profit.

When William Cobbett, writing in the early nineteenth century, railed against the plight of English farmers and warned of their imminent disappearance, as tenants were driven off the land by rents they could not afford, and labourers were paid starvation wages, he was certainly registering a reality. But, while he was recording a very particular and in many ways decisive crisis in the English countryside, in the wake of the Napoleonic wars and in the throes of industrialization, the historical dynamic at the heart of that crisis had begun long before and continues to this day.

Just as Cobbett's lament has precursors in sixteenth-century protests against enclosure, we can hear its echoes today. Yet again, we are hearing predictions that the current agricultural crisis will be the last straw for the beleaguered British farmer and the end of small farms, this time driven to the wall by the largest producers working in tandem with the supermarket chains – and supported by government. And as some angry British farmers try their luck across the Channel, we can even hear again Cobbett's warning about desperate farmers carrying 'their allegiance, their capital (what they have left), and their skill to go and grease the fat sow, our old friends the Bourbons'.[2]

WAS AGRARIAN CAPITALISM REALLY CAPITALIST?

We should pause here to emphasize two major points. First, it was not merchants or manufacturers who drove the process that propelled the early development of capitalism. The transformation of social property relations was firmly rooted in the countryside, and the transformation of English trade and industry was result more than cause of England's transition to capitalism. Merchants could function perfectly well within non-capitalist systems. They prospered, as we have seen, in the context of European feudalism, where they profited not only from the autonomy of cities but also from the fragmentation of markets and the opportunity to conduct transactions between one market and another.

Secondly, and even more fundamentally, the term 'agrarian capitalism' has so far been used without placing wage labour at its core, although by any definition wage labour is central to capitalism. This requires some explanation.

It should be said that many English tenants did employ wage labour, so much so that the triad identified by Marx and others – landlords living on capitalist ground rent, capitalist tenants living on profit, and labourers living on wages – has been regarded by many as the defining characteristic of agrarian relations in England. And so it was, at least in those parts of the country, particularly in the south and south-east, most noted for their agricultural productivity. The new economic pressures, the competitive pressures that drove unproductive farmers to the wall, were a major factor in polarizing the agrarian population into larger landholders and propertyless wage labourers, promoting the agrarian triad. And, of course, the pressures to increase productivity made themselves felt in the intensified exploitation of wage labour.

It would not, then, be unreasonable to define English agrarian capitalism in terms of the triad. But it is important to keep in mind that competitive pressures, and the new 'laws of motion' that went with them, depended in the first instance not on the existence of a mass proletariat but on the existence of market-dependent tenant-producers. Wage labourers, and especially those who depended entirely on wages for their livelihood and not just for seasonal supplements (the kind of seasonal and supplementary wage labour that has existed since ancient times in peasant societies), remained very much a minority in seventeenth-century England.

Besides, these competitive pressures affected not just tenants who employed wage labourers but also farmers who – typically with their families – were themselves direct producers working without hired labour. People could be market-dependent –

dependent on the market for the basic conditions of their self-reproduction – without being completely dispossessed. To be market-dependent required only the loss of direct non-market access to the means of self-reproduction, and specifically land. Once market imperatives were well established, even outright ownership was no protection against them. Market dependence was a cause, not a result, of mass proletarianization.

In other words, the specific dynamics we associate with capitalism were already in place in English agriculture before the proletarianization of the workforce. In fact, those dynamics were a major factor in bringing about the proletarianization of labour in England. The critical factor was the market dependence of producers, as well as appropriators, and the new social imperatives created by that market dependence.

Some people may be reluctant to describe this social formation as 'capitalist' on the grounds that capitalism is, by definition, based on the exploitation of wage labour. That reluctance is fair enough, as long as we recognize that, whatever we call it, the English economy in the early modern period, driven by the logic of its basic productive sector, agriculture, was already operating according to principles and 'laws of motion' different from those prevailing in any other society since the dawn of history. Those laws of motion were the *preconditions* – which existed nowhere else – for the development of a mature capitalism that would indeed be based on the mass exploitation of wage labour.

What, then, was the outcome of all this? First, English agriculture was distinctively productive. By the end of the seventeenth century, for instance, grain and cereal production had risen so dramatically that England became for a time a leading exporter of those commodities. These advances in production were achieved with a relatively small agricultural labour force. This is what it means to speak of the distinctive *productivity* of English agriculture.

In Part I, we encountered the dismissal of English 'agrarian capitalism' on the grounds that the 'productivity' of French agriculture in the eighteenth century was more or less equal to that of England. But in France it took more units of labour to produce the same output, while English agriculture was able to sustain a larger proportion of people not engaged in agricultural production with a smaller workforce, in a declining rural population. The issue, again, is not total output but labour-productivity, output per unit of work.

The demographic facts alone speak volumes. It is not uncommon to argue that England's agricultural productivity, because it was capable of sustaining a population explosion, helped to fuel industrialization. But by the time England's population density began to eclipse that of other countries in Western Europe, when their population growth had levelled off if not declined, the pattern of English economic development was already distinctive. A demographic increase may help to explain the development of industrial capitalism, but it cannot explain the emergence of capitalism itself. If anything, that population explosion was effect rather than cause. But even before a unique pattern of population increase became manifest in England, its demographic composition was already distinct in other significant ways, which tell us a great deal about English economic development.

Between 1500 and 1700, English population growth, though substantial like that of other European countries, was in some respects distinctive. The percentage of its urban population more than doubled in that period (some historians put the urban percentage at just under a quarter of the total population already by the late seventeenth century). Although the urban population had not reached the levels of the Dutch Republic, the contrast with France is telling. There, the rural population remained fairly stable, still about 85 to 90 percent at the time of the French Revolution in 1789 and beyond. By 1850, when the urban population of England and Wales was about 40.8 per cent, France's was still only 14.4 per cent (and Germany's 10.8).[3]

So already in the early modern period, British agriculture was productive enough to sustain an unusually large number of people no longer engaged in agricultural production. As we have seen, this distinguished it even from the Dutch Republic, which, although the proportion of its urban population was even larger, depended on its pre-eminent role in international trade to sustain not only its huge urban population but even its agricultural producers. In other words, as productive as Dutch agriculture was, the capacity of the Dutch economy to feed a large urban population was disproportionately dependent on international trade and circulating goods produced elsewhere.

The distinctive British – and, more specifically, English – situation testifies, of course, to more than just particularly efficient farming techniques. It also bespeaks a revolution in social property relations. While France, for instance, remained a country of peasant proprietors, land in England was concentrated in far fewer hands, and the propertyless mass was growing rapidly. The central issue, however, is not the size of holdings. While agricultural production in France still followed traditional peasant practices (nothing like the English body of improvement literature existed in France, and the village community still imposed its regulations and restrictions on production, even affecting larger landholders), English farming was responding to the imperatives of competition and improvement.[4]

There was something even more distinctive about England's demographic pattern. The growth of the urban population was not evenly distributed among English towns. Elsewhere in Europe, the typical pattern was an urban population scattered among several important towns – so that, for example, Lyons was not dwarfed by Paris. London, however, became disproportion-ately huge compared to other English towns, growing from about 60,000 inhabitants around 1530 to 575,000 in 1700 and becoming the largest city in Europe.

This pattern signifies more than is apparent at first glance. It testifies, among other things, to the transformation of social property relations in the heartland of agrarian capitalism, the south and south-east, and the dispossession of small producers, whose destination as displaced migrants would typically be

London. The growth of London also represents the growing unification not only of the English state but also of a national market. That huge city was the hub of English commerce. It was both a major transit point for national and international trade and a vast consumer of English products, not least its agricultural produce. The growth of London, in other words, in all kinds of ways stands for England's emerging capitalism: its increasingly single, unified, integrated, and competitive market; its productive agriculture; and its dispossessed population.

MARKET DEPENDENCE AND A NEW COMMERCIAL SYSTEM

The distinctive and unprecedented logic of agrarian capitalism made itself felt in every sphere of economic life. It is certainly true that English capitalism emerged in the context of a larger trading system and would not have emerged without that. But contrary to conventions that find the driving force of economic development in commercial activity, the economic 'laws of motion' born in the English countryside transformed the age-old rules of trade and created an entirely new kind of commercial system.

While other major commercial powers in Europe had developed on the strength of foreign trade, the kind of carrying trade described by Polanyi, British capitalism depended on a highly developed domestic market, with a growing population no longer engaged in producing everyday goods – like food and textiles – for their own and their families' consumption. The massive London market for basic consumer goods was the hub of this growing domestic market, a market that differed from others in size, substance, and 'laws of motion'. The increasingly national, integrated nature of that market meant that it was increasingly operating not simply on the principles of 'profit on alienation' but also on the basis of competitive production.

England even developed its own distinctive banking system. Other major European trading centres had banking systems that had evolved in ancient and medieval times: moneychanging operations, public banks dealing with state finances and currency regulation, and mechanisms for financing foreign and long-distance trade. England was relatively weak in banking of this 'classical' kind, but it created a new banking system that originated, in contrast to the rest of Europe, in domestic trade, largely in domestic products. This system was rooted not in foreign trade, 'not in commercial arbitrage between separate markets', but in the 'metropolitan market' centred on London, to facilitate a network of distribution from the capital outwards throughout the country by means of 'factors' or agents who operated on commissions and credits.[5] It is not difficult to see that this distinctive financial and commercial system had its roots in agrarian capitalism, in the changing social relations that produced both a need for such a market to sustain a growing non-agrarian population and the capacity to meet that need.

The dynamics of the English domestic market expanded outward into international trade. The developing national economy was also becoming the centre of an international commercial system different from any trading system before it. Just as the old network of local markets and the 'carrying' trade between them were giving way to an integrated market, a system of world commerce originating in Britain, and especially in London, was emerging that would replace 'the infinite succession of arbitrage operations between separate, distinct, and discrete markets that had previously constituted foreign trade'.[6] The characteristic instruments produced by the English domestic commercial system, bills of exchange and especially the 'bills on London', also became the instruments of international trade. When England gained unambiguous ascendancy in international commerce, in what is sometimes called the 'commercial capitalism' of the eighteenth century, its success was built on the foundations of the earlier domestic commercial system; and even the military power, the massive naval power, that secured British pre-eminence was clearly rooted in the wealth created by agrarian capitalism.

The commercial system associated with the development of agrarian capitalism was distinctively rooted in domestic production and consumption. This was the first, and for a long time the only, commercial system based on production of the means of survival and self-reproduction for a growing mass market.[7] This is not to deny the importance, in the larger European commercial system, of trade in basic necessities of the kind we encountered in our discussion of the grain trade. But the British, and more particularly the English, created a new kind of commercial system, driven by different needs and answering to a logic different from any other in history. To be sure, they participated in the old commercial system, and they certainly experienced a consumer boom in luxury goods. Nor, of course, can it be denied that the wealth of prosperous classes continued to play – as, by definition, it must, in any grossly unequal society, including, and especially, capitalism – an economic role disproportionate to their numbers in all forms of trade. But alongside the more traditional forms of trade, there emerged, in England's domestic market, a novel system with a logic of its own, which eventually extended its reach beyond Britain's national boundaries to create a new system of international trade.

Again, the English domestic market was, already by the seventeenth century, something like a unified national market, without the disjunctions that had characterized international trade (disjunctions that, indeed, have yet to be entirely overcome even by today's 'globalization'), and without the internal trade barriers that still affected domestic economies elsewhere, not just fragmented city-states but even a centralized kingdom like France. This national economy was also increasingly distinctive in the sheer size and the particular composition of the market for basic necessities, as well as for simple, cheap commodities of everyday life, like iron cooking pots. The decline of the English peasantry may have taken longer than has sometimes been suggested, extending well into the nineteenth century. But as the early market dependence of English tenant farmers, already visible in the sixteenth century in the form of competitive rents, accelerated the dispossession of those unable to survive in increasingly competitive conditions, market dependence increasingly took the more complete form of commodified labour-power and the reliance on a wage for access to the means of subsistence.

The European grain trade had traditionally been directed largely to urban populations, which, of course, grew substantially in the relevant period. It is true, as we have seen, that the proportion of urban to rural populations in England increased more than most, and London became the largest city in Europe, a uniquely huge consumer of basic necessities. But this demographic pattern alone was not enough to account for the uniqueness of England's domestic market. The even larger proportion of urban to rural populations in the Dutch Republic, for instance, did not have the same effect.[8] Yet there is a telling contrast between these two cases that may tell us more. The urban population in the Dutch Golden Age was swelled not simply by the poor and dispossessed unable to sustain themselves on agricultural production but also to an unusual degree by those who benefited from or serviced the Republic's great commercial wealth. By contrast, the English city, London in particular, was disproportionately enlarged by the poor dispossessed by agrarian capitalism. In any case, what made the English market for basic goods distinctive was not simply the demographic distribution between town and country but also the growing proportion of the population, whether urban or rural, that was dispossessed and reliant on wages for survival, together with the more direct relation of production to consumption of this kind.

Historians have devoted much attention to the growth of a 'consumer society' in Britain (as well as elsewhere, notably in the Netherlands).[9] There can be little doubt that, particularly in the eighteenth century and especially with the growth of prosperous urban classes, there was a burgeoning market for all kinds of goods beyond the basic necessities, from fine apparel to works of art. But the 'consumer society' in England, however new it may have been in the size of the market and the range of its goods, was not qualitatively different from bourgeois markets elsewhere in Europe. Nor were such consumer markets fundamentally discontinuous from Europe's medieval burgher culture, and their sheer quantitative growth was not enough to distinguish them fundamentally from the luxury trade of earlier periods. To identify what was truly new and distinctive, representing a major qualitative break from old economic patterns and the operation of a new systemic logic, we have to look elsewhere.

It can be misleading to define the specific character of the new economy in Britain by stressing the growing wealth of the 'middle classes' or the numbers of consumers who were *able* to buy a wide range of goods to enhance their comfort, pleasure, aesthetic enjoyment, or status. More distinctive was the growth of the numbers *compelled* to buy – not the superfluities of life but the most basic commodities and the implements of daily subsistence and self-reproduction. Needless to say, the growth of such a market presupposed the *ability* to buy no less than the compulsion. In the historical moment between agrarian and industrial capitalism, the purchasing power of labourers may indeed have been unusually substantial, and no doubt the definition of necessity was becoming ever more elastic, increasingly embracing manufactured instruments of daily life such as industrially produced kitchenware and eating utensils. But *compulsion* lies at the heart of the new economic dynamic; and, in this kind of market, even the ability to buy was defined by its strict limitations. It was certainly a novelty that so many working people were now consumers, but the specific logic of this novel market depended as much on the poverty of its consumers as the luxury trade depended on wealth.

It is not, however, enough to say that first England and then Britain saw the emergence of a historically unprecedented mass market for cheap everyday commodities. What finally distinguishes this market from earlier markets in basic necessities is the fact that, in the context of capitalist property relations, the consumption needs of relatively poor consumers became the driving force of a new kind of market also in the sense that this market affected production in wholly new ways. The new patterns of consumption directly affected production as never before, in the context of an already integrated and increasingly competitive national market. English agricultural production in the age of agrarian capitalism substantially supplied its own domestic market for food, and, as we have seen, England was, for a time, even a net exporter of grain. At the same time, the development of productive forces in the countryside was the corollary of transformations in social property relations that eventually also created the mass of wage-earning consumers. English agriculture was sufficiently productive by itself – not only, like the Dutch, by means of exchange, dependent on a super-abundance of purely commercial wealth – to sustain a large population no longer engaged in agricultural production, while British industry developed on the strength of cheap basic goods, like cotton cloth, and their accessibility to that growing mass market.

The development of a mass proletariat employed by capital represented the ultimate development of the direct relationship between production and consumption. (It also, of course, represented a fundamental contradiction: the same conditions that brought about the integration of production and consumption, the same forces that overcame the disjunctions of the old commercial system, the same imperatives of competition and capital accumulation, with their systematic tendency to overcapacity, also ensured a regular imbalance between production and consumption, a new and systematic disjunction between supply and demand. In the old commercial system, with its spatial and structural disconnections between production and consumption, between supply and demand, there could certainly be imbalances, but they were, so to speak, contingent, arising by default rather than by compulsion. The absence of the imperatives of competition meant that there were no systemic mechanisms that *compelled* the regular recurrence of such imbalances, least of all the imbalances of overcapacity.) The proletariat constituted both a force of production and a mass consumer market, and the condition of the proletariat in both its aspects shaped the development of productive forces.

In a competitive environment with systemic imperatives to increase labour-productivity, the general commodification of labour-power in the form of wage labour compelled capital, already driven by competitive pressures, to extract the maximum surplus value from workers in the limited time during which it controlled the labour-power of those juridically free workers. At the same time, these propertyless wage labourers, dependent on the market for all their material needs, determined the nature of production not only by their own productive activity but also by their powers of consumption.

This kind of consumption constituted a market uniquely broad and inclusive, but also uniquely limited in its resources. As a class entirely dependent on exchanging a money-wage for the most basic means of subsistence, the proletariat represented a larger market in a more or less unified geographic space, and in a more or less integrated economy, than had ever existed before. But it was also a market whose consumers had restricted powers of consumption. That distinctive combination naturally engendered its own pressures for cost-effective production. Production for this market required making up in numbers what consumers lacked in wealth, and this created pressures to produce cheaply, pressures that reinforced the cost-sensitivity imposed by already existing imperatives of competition and the need to invest in the technical means of improving labour-productivity. This was, in other words, the first economic system in history in which the *limitations* of the market impelled instead of inhibiting the forces of production.

Until the *production* of the means of survival and self-reproduction is market-dependent, there is no capitalist mode of production. With the advent of industrial capitalism, market dependence had truly penetrated to the depths of the social order. But its precondition was an already well-established and deeply rooted market dependence, reaching back to the early days of English agrarian capitalism, when the production of food became subject to the imperatives of competition. This was a unique social form in which the main economic actors, both appropriators and producers, were market-dependent in historically unprecedented ways.

The market dependence of English farmers was based not simply on the need to exchange in order to obtain goods they could not produce but also on the particular relation between 'economic' tenants and landlords devoid of extra-economic powers. Even the productive capacity to be self-sufficient in agriculture would not make producers in England less market-dependent. Theirs was a particularly stringent, all-or-nothing mode of market dependence, which was in no way alleviated by more than adequate productive capacities.

The English situation, then, was distinctive in several related ways. The producer's access to land itself was directly determined by the market, and the degree of market success required in order to retain possession was not determined by the producer himself, by the needs of his family, or by their own consumption patterns – or, for that matter, by their own hunger for profit. Possession of good and ample land did not eliminate or even reduce dependence on the market. On the contrary, dependence on the market – by means of economic leases – was a condition for access to that kind of land; and more successful farmers were likely to have more access to more land. So producers who had the *possibility* to compete and maximize profit were likely to be those who were most subject to the *need* to do so. That compulsion derived in the first instance from their relation to appropriators who themselves lacked non-market access to the means of appropriation, landlords who relied on *economic* modes of surplus extraction. In that way, profit – not direct consumption or exchange – became the immediate object of production, and for the first time in history there developed a mode of exploitation that systematically impelled the development of productive forces.

FROM AGRARIAN TO INDUSTRIAL CAPITALISM

The long-term consequences of England's agrarian capitalism for subsequent economic development should be fairly obvious. Although this is not the place to explore in detail the connections between agrarian capitalism and England's development into the first 'industrialized' economy, some points are self-evident. We can at least outline the ways in which industrial capitalism presupposed its agrarian form.

Without a productive agricultural sector that could sustain a large non-agricultural workforce, the world's first industrial capitalism would have been unlikely to emerge. Without England's agrarian capitalism, there would have been no dispossessed mass obliged to sell its labour-power for a wage. Without that dispossessed non-agrarian workforce, there would have been no mass consumer market for the cheap everyday goods – such as food and textiles – that drove the process of industrialization in England. It is worth emphasizing that this large market derived its special character not only from its unusual size but also from its limitations, the relative poverty of consumers demanding cheap goods for everyday use. It had more in common with later mass consumer markets than with the luxury trade of 'classical' commerce.

Finally (this is no doubt a more contentious point), without English capitalism there would probably have been no capitalist system of any kind: it was competitive pressures emanating from England, especially an industrialized England, that, in the first instance, compelled other countries to promote their own economic development in capitalist directions. States still acting on pre-capitalist principles of trade, or geopolitical and military rivalry hardly different in principle from older, feudal conflicts over territory and plunder, would be driven by England's new competitive advantages to promote their own economic development in similar ways.[10]

At the very least, agrarian capitalism made industrialization possible. To say even this much is already to say a great deal. The conditions of possibility created by agrarian capitalism – the transformations in property relations, in the size and nature of the domestic market, in the composition of the population, and in the nature and extent of British trade and British imperialism – were more substantial and far-reaching than any purely technological advances required by industrialization. This is true in two senses: first, purely technological advances, again, were not responsible for the so-called 'agricultural revolution' that laid the foundation of industrialization; and second, the technological changes that constituted the first 'Industrial Revolution' were in any case modest.[11]

Whether agrarian capitalism made industrial capitalism not only possible but also necessary or inevitable is another question, but there was a strong historical impulse in that direction. An integrated market providing cheap necessities of life for a growing mass of consumers and responding to already well-established competitive pressures created a new and specific 'logic of process', the outcome of which was industrial capitalism. That market, and the social property relations in which it was rooted, provided not only the means but also the need to produce consumer goods on a new scale, and also to produce them cost-effectively, in ways determined by the imperatives of competition, accumulation, and profit-maximization, together with their requirements for improving labour-productivity.

In other words, in contrast to Polanyi's suggestion that 'market society' was a response to certain technological developments in a commercial society, the conclusion we can draw from the history of agrarian capitalism is that a capitalist dynamic rooted in a new form of social property relations preceded industrialization, both chronologically and causally. In fact, a kind of 'market society' – in which producers were dependent on the market for access to the means of life, labour, and self-reproduction, and subject to market imperatives – was not the *result* of industrialization but its primary cause. Only a transformation in social property relations that compelled people to produce competitively (and not just to buy cheap and sell dear), a transformation that made access to the means of self-reproduction dependent on the market, can explain the dramatic revolutionizing of productive forces uniquely characteristic of modern capitalism.

Industrialization was, then, the result not the cause of market society, and capitalist laws of motion were the cause not the result of mass proletarianization. But that, of course, was not the end of capitalist development. Proletarianization, which meant the complete commodification of labour-power, would confer new and more far-reaching coercive powers on the market by creating a working class that was completely market-dependent and completely vulnerable to market disciplines, with no mediations and no alternative resources. While both capital and labour were in their various ways subject to the impersonal forces of the market, the market itself would become increasingly a major axis of class division between exploiters and exploited, between buyers and sellers of labour-power. In that sense, it was a new coercive instrument for capital, the ultimate discipline in its control of labour, and a new terrain of class struggle.

No doubt other societies, especially England's commercial rivals, relied on trade to supply certain basic conditions of subsistence. But in none of them was production subject to the pressures of market dependence in the same way. More particularly, in none of them was access to the very means of agricultural production, to land, market-dependent as it was in the conditions of English property relations; and in none of them was appropriation market-dependent in the way that it was for English propertied classes already from the early modern period.

The effect of the English system was not only to make agricultural producers and landed appropriators uniquely subject to market imperatives and the requirements of competitive production, but also to propel the mass dispossession that created both the labour force and the market for wholly new forms of industrial production. The end result was a system of production, with mutually reinforcing agrarian and industrial sectors, uniquely capable of imposing its competitive imperatives on other parts of the world; and with it came a new commercial system. Thereafter, and especially with the advent of British industrial capitalism, economic development elsewhere, from Britain's European neighbours to the farthest corners of the colonial world, would be determined by the new imperatives of capitalism.

Once the first capitalism assumed its industrial form, the market as a means of exchange and circulation did indeed become a transmission belt for capitalist competitive pressures. From then on, economies inserted in the international trading system and depending on it for their material needs, whatever their prevailing social property relations, would be subject to capitalist imperatives.

Although the origin of capitalism depended on the social relation between market-dependent producers and appropriators, once commodification and competition became a virtually universal form of social reproduction, producers even in the absence of class exploitation were subject to market imperatives. This was true of independent farmers and would have been no less true of independent workers' industrial collectives. Those imperatives, in turn, would carry in their wake strong pressures to transform social property relations, to reproduce the class relation between capital and labour; and as the process of capitalist development took its course, with mass dispossession and the general commodification of labour-power, there developed wholly new and even more inescapable imperatives of competition and capital accumulation.

The capitalist system is, needless to say, in a constant state of development and flux. But we will not understand its current processes of change and contradiction if we fail to trace them to their foundations. The rise of capitalism cannot be explained as the outcome of technical improvements, 'the Western European trend of economic progress', or any other transhistorical mechanism. The specific transformation of social property relations that *set in train* a historically unique 'progress' of productive forces cannot be taken for granted. To acknowledge this is critical to an understanding of capitalism – not to mention the conditions of its abolition and replacement by a different social form. We must recognize not only the full force of capitalist imperatives, the compulsions of accumulation, profit-maximization, and increasing labour-productivity, but also their systemic roots, so we know just why they work the way they do.

7

THE ORIGIN OF
CAPITALIST IMPERIALISM

All the major powers in sixteenth- and seventeenth-century Europe were deeply engaged in colonial ventures, conquest, plunder, and imperial oppression. Yet these ventures were associated with very different patterns of economic development, only one of which was capitalist. In fact, the one unambiguous case of capitalist development, England, was notoriously slow in embarking on overseas colonization, or even dominating trade routes; and the development of its distinctive social property relations was already well underway by the time it became a major contender in the colonial race. So the connection between capitalism and imperialism is far from simple and straightforward.

PRE-CAPITALIST IMPERIALISM

A common account of the connection between imperialism and capitalism, often associated with left versions of the commercialization model, suggests that European imperialist ventures in the New World, Africa, and Asia were decisive in the process of 'primitive accumulation' leading to capitalism. Imperialism permitted 'proto-capitalists' in Europe to accumulate the critical mass of wealth required to make the leap forward that distinguished 'the West' from other societies that until then had been more advanced in commercial, technological, and cultural development. At the same time, imperialist exploitation drained the resources and halted the development of non-European economies.

Some versions of this explanation emphasize the importance of wealth amassed from the New World, in the form of gold and silver. Here, the critical – or at least emblematic – date is 1492, when Columbus sailed (inadvertently) to the Americas. Others stress the importance of the later slave trade and the wealth derived from slave plantations, in particular for the trade in sugar. Still others single out the importance of the British Empire in India in the process of industrialization.[1]

Yet we cannot get very far in explaining the rise of capitalism by invoking the contribution of imperialism to 'primitive accumulation' or, indeed, by attributing to it any decisive role in the *origin* of capitalism. Not only did British overseas colonization lag behind the imperialist ventures of its European rivals, its acquisition of colonial wealth also lagged behind its own domestic capitalist development. By contrast, Spain, the dominant early colonial power and the leader in 'primitive accumulation' of the classical kind, which amassed huge wealth especially from South American mines, and was well endowed with 'capital' in the simple sense of wealth, did not develop in a capitalist direction. Instead, it expended its massive colonial wealth in essentially feudal pursuits, especially war as a means of extra-economic appropriation, and the construction of its Habsburg empire in Europe. Having overextended and overtaxed its European empire, it went into a deep and long-term decline in the seventeenth and eighteenth centuries.

Nor is it a simple matter to trace the causal connections between imperialism and the later development of industrial capitalism. Marxist historians, for instance, have forcefully argued, against many arguments to the contrary, that the greatest crime of European empire, slavery, made a major contribution to the development of industrial capitalism.[2] But here, too, we have to keep in mind that Britain was not alone in exploiting colonial slavery and that elsewhere it had different effects. Other major

European powers amassed great wealth from slavery and from the trade in sugar or in addictive goods like tobacco, which, it has been argued, fuelled the trade in living human beings.[3] But, again, only in Britain was that wealth converted into industrial capital.

So we are still left with the question of why colonialism was associated with capitalism in one case and not another. Even those who are less interested in the origin of capitalism than in the 'Industrial Revolution', at a time when Britain really had become a pre-eminent imperial power, still have to explain why imperialism produced industrial capitalism in this case and not in others.

It is very hard to avoid the conclusion that much, if not everything, depended on the social property relations at home in the imperial power, the particular conditions of systemic repro-duction associated with those property relations, and the particular economic processes set in motion by them. The wealth amassed from colonial exploitation may have contributed substantially to further development, even if it was not a necessary precondition of the *origin* of capitalism. And once British capitalism, especially in its industrial form, was well established, it was able to impose capitalist imperatives on other economies with different social property relations. But no amount of colonial wealth would have had these effects without the imperatives generated by England's domestic property relations. If wealth from the colonies and the slave trade contributed to Britain's industrial revolution, it was because the British economy had already for a long time been structured by capitalist social property relations. By contrast, the truly enormous wealth accumulated by Spain and Portugal had no such effect because they were unambiguously non-capitalist economies.

We can, nevertheless, indentify a specifically capitalist form of imperialism, an imperialism that was more the result than the cause of capitalist development and stands in contrast to other European forms. So let us, first, sketch out in very broad strokes the traditional, pre-capitalist modes of imperialism and the way they were related to pre-capitalist social property relations at home in the imperial power.

As we have seen, in pre-capitalist societies, appropriation – whether just to meet the material needs of society or to enhance the wealth of exploiters – took, so to speak, an absolute form: squeezing more out of direct producers rather than enhancing the productivity of labour. That is to say, as a general rule pre-capitalist exploitation took place by 'extra-economic' means, by means of direct coercion, using military, political, and juridical powers to extract surpluses from direct producers who typically remained in possession of the means of production. For that reason, too, relations of economic exploitation between classes were inseparable from 'non-economic' relations like the political relations between rulers and subjects. As for trade in these societies, it generally took the form of profit on alienation, buying cheap and selling dear, typically in separate markets, depending more on extra-economic advantages of various kinds than on competitive production.

Imperial expansion tended to follow the same logic. In some cases, it was largely an extension of coercive, extra-economic, absolute appropriation: using military power to squeeze taxes and tribute out of subject territories; seizing more territory and resources; capturing and enslaving human beings. In other cases, it was conducted in the interests of non-capitalist commerce, where profits were derived from a carrying trade or from arbitrage among many separate markets. In cases like this, extra-economic power might be used to secure trade routes, to impose monopolies, to gain exclusive rights to some precious commodity, and so on.

Consider some of the typical patterns of European colonialism in the early modern period. Much of it has to do not with the settlement of colonies by people from the metropolis but rather with gaining control of important trade routes or trading monopolies, or cornering the supply of some precious commodity. The

Spanish empire in the Americas, long the dominant European overseas empire, was less concerned even with commerce than with amassing bullion, extracting its wealth from the gold and silver mines of South America. So dependent did the Spanish economy become on this treasure that many observers from the beginning have argued that this preoccupation at the expense of commerce or agricultural production obstructed Spain's economic development.

Where there was settlement, it tended to be for the purpose of enhancing trade, whether by establishing trading posts or by means of more wide-ranging territorial occupation. This kind of settlement might have little to do with production, or production might be for the purpose of provisioning the imperial power's merchant ships – as was the case with the Cape Colony established by the Dutch in southern Africa.

Another example of pre-capitalist empire was the French colonization of Canada, where the principal economic objective was the fur trade. At the same time, a type of settler colony was established that seems to have had no immediate economic function. The *seigneuries* of New France constituted a subsistence economy, deliberately (if loosely) modelled on feudalism. Whatever purpose they may have served for the mother country, there was nothing here, either in the form of the settlements or in their purpose, that suggests any association with, or predisposition to, capitalist development.

In other cases, where production was developed as an adjunct to trade, it tended to be based on pre-capitalist modes of extra-economic exploitation: in particular, the slave plantation, which several European powers favoured, especially in pursuit of the massive trade in sugar, or the Spanish *encomienda* system, which amounted to the enslavement of indigenous peoples. Needless to say, capitalism did not put an end to these old imperial practices. On the contrary, it created new reasons, new needs, for pursuing some of them with even greater gusto, especially slavery. But the point is that it created a whole new logic of its own, new forms of appropriation and exploitation with their own rules and requirements, and with that came a new imperial dynamic, which affected even older forms of exploitation.

IRELAND: A NEW CAPITALIST IMPERIALISM?

The new dynamics of a growing capitalist system produced a new form of colonization and a new kind of imperial drive: not just the age-old hunger for wealth and plunder but, more specifically, an outward expansion of the same capitalist imperatives that were driving the domestic market, the imperatives of competitive production and capital accumulation.

Capitalist imperatives also created new motives and justifications for coercive dispossession. In pre-capitalist societies, land with labour attached to it, labour accessible to extra-economic coercion, is generally more valuable than land by itself. Command over people is more immediately important than direct command over land. The Spanish empire, for instance, in its pursuit of South American treasure, while it was unquestionably genocidal, made ample use of indigenous populations and their technical expertise. In capitalism, these is certainly a need for a labour force, but where competitive pressure to increase labour-productivity is the driving imperative, there are entirely new reasons for concentrating property, and entirely new reasons for dispossessing direct producers. In England, for instance, this had the added effect of creating a dispossessed surplus population of potential colonial settlers – and it is easy to see the difference here between England and a peasant society like France, which never produced that kind of surplus population.

England's relations with Ireland in the early modern period provide an insight into the dynamics of early capitalist imperialism. The social processes and ideological strategies associated with English agrarian capitalism were clearly manifest here, and the case of Ireland serves as an illuminating introduction to the emerging differences between capitalist imperialism and earlier forms. The processes we are concerned with took place from the Tudor colonization in the sixteenth century, to Cromwell's conquest in the mid-seventeenth century. There had already been a long history of English invasion and attempts to subdue the 'wild Irish', but a significant shift occurred in the late sixteenth century. Just at the time when the Tudor monarchy was consolidating the state in England, it also set out to impose that state's hegemony on Ireland, and it is revealing to see the changes in its strategies of control.

There had long been attempts to subdue Ireland by direct military means, and in the sixteenth century, there were various unsuccessful efforts to establish private military settlements as a defence against Irish rebellion. This was, in effect, a feudal model of imperial domination, with a kind of feudal lordship being used to dominate a dependent population by extra-economic means. The Tudor monarchy sought to extend its rule over Ireland by force in a more systematic way, dominated by the state, but it also tried something new, which was to have far-reaching implications for the development of British imperialism.

In the late sixteenth century, England's Irish strategy underwent something like an instant transition from feudalism to capitalism. The Tudor state decided to embark on a more aggressive process of colonization. But this time, the effort to exert extra-economic control by a more effective military conquest was supplemented by an attempt to impose a kind of *economic* hegemony, using military force to implant a new economic system, as well as a new political and legal order.

In 1585, for instance, the English government announced a plan to re-create the conditions of south-east England in Munster by granting expropriated lands to settlers who would introduce English agriculture to the region. The object was not, of course, simply to introduce particular crops or techniques. The very conscious intention was to establish an English-style commercial order, a new kind of economy based on new social relations on the land, new relations between landlord and tenant, like the ones that were driving improvement in England. In other words, as an adjunct to direct means of military suppression, the new imperial project of the English state was to subdue the Irish by transforming their social property relations and introducing agrarian capitalism. Needless to say, the most effective means of achieving this transformation was still outright domination of the Irish or their complete eviction from their lands. But even if Ireland were not successfully absorbed into the English state, it could be integrated into England's economic orbit and subject to its economic coercions, as an extension of the English economy.

The English embarked on forcible expropriation of the Irish and resettlement of their lands by Englishmen and Scots, with or without Irish tenants. Military violence, reaching its brutal peak in the middle of the next century with Cromwell's conquest, would continue to be an indispensable instrument of empire. But the effect of the new strategy was also to compel Irish chieftains themselves to adapt to the transplanted commercial economy, and to adopt English landlord–tenant relations, to become improving – and expropriating – landlords, and even to encourage the settlement of Englishmen and Scots as tenants on their land. No doubt this was partly the age-old effect of subject elites emulating and ingratiating themselves with imperial overlords, but there were surely also some purely economic compulsions at work, the imperatives of economic competition. The consequence of this attempt to transform the dominant property relations, and to enrich the imperial masters by this means, was to impoverish the vast numbers who were dispossessed and pushed to the margins of the new system.

The intention was not to turn Ireland into a commercial competitor, even for the benefit of colonial settlers. It was rather to make Ireland an economic dependency of England, exploitable in the interests of the metropolitan power. As soon as Irish commercial expansion became a competitive threat, as it showed signs of doing in the seventeenth century, the English imposed restrictions that thwarted development – in a pattern that would repeat itself throughout the imperial history of capitalism. This history exemplifies one of the founding contradictions of capitalism: the need to impose its imperatives as universally as possible, and the need to limit the damaging consequences that this universalization has for capital itself.

The Irish experience became, quite consciously, a model of empire for the English. The 'aggressive colonialism' pioneered here by the Tudor state 'was the chief legacy of late Elizabethan Ireland to English colonization in the New World'.[4] Even some of the same personnel found their way to the Americas, and beyond. Englishmen schooled in the Irish colonial venture transported their experience to the American colonies, not to mention the Scots, whose role in Ireland was only the beginning of a long tradition of service to the British Empire. For the Irish themselves, expropriation, from very early on, often meant migration to the colonies. Even some Irish Catholic planters learned the imperial lesson all too well, settling in the West Indies, for instance, and helping to bring indentured servants from Ireland to boost the labour force. Especially after the massive evictions of the Cromwellian conquest, the Irish may have constituted the largest single white migration to the West Indies in the seventeenth century.

The Irish model, then, represented a pattern of imperial settlement different from other European empires, a form of colonial domination that replaced existing property relations with new ones driven by market imperatives. The social transformation typically took the form of violent expropriation, and, especially in the New World, even genocide. But even in the absence of direct colonial rule, or at least in the absence of successful direct domination, it might now be possible to impose a new economic order with coercions of its own – perhaps the world's first structural adjustment programmes.

Later developments in the British Empire, especially in Asia and Africa, would produce a variety of imperial forms, some quite different from the early colonial settlements. Where, as especially in India, the imperial state confronted a densely populated and economically advanced power, with deeply rooted and complex political arrangements, methods and ideologies had to be found that would enable and justify the domination of one powerful state by another. Needless to say, military force and conquest always remained central to the imperial project, with or without settler colonies. While white settler colonies did persist in various places, the model pioneered in Ireland was eclipsed by other forms. Still, there are ways in which that model presaged the future form of capitalist imperialism, and some of its principles have survived to this day. Dispossession and extinction of traditional property rights, of one kind or another, have, of course, been a continuing practice; but most of all, capitalism has developed to its utmost limit the practice of economic compulsion, as distinct from direct political and military coercion, not only as a mode of class rule but also as a form of imperial domination.

In today's 'globalized' economy, old forms of military subjugation and direct rule have been largely replaced by the imposition of economic compulsions, the imperatives of the capitalist market manipulated in the interests of a few imperial powers, and one in particular. To be sure, behind the new global economic order is the most powerful military force the world has ever seen, and the constant threat of military coercion by the US, with or without the cover of 'international' cooperation, is a necessary bulwark of 'globalization'. But today, the old role of colonial settlers as a means of transporting economic compulsions has been taken over by local nation states, which act as transmission belts for capitalist imperatives and enforce the 'laws' of the market.

EMPIRE AND THE IDEOLOGY
OF IMPROVEMENT

In the seventeenth century, the new logic of capitalism was becoming more transparent and, as we have seen, was finding increasingly explicit ideological and theoretical expression. In particular, as increasing labour-productivity became the overriding imperative, that imperative made its way into new conceptions of property rights. Making land productive – that is, *improving* it – was becoming the basis of property rights; and, more particularly, the *failure* to improve could mean *forfeiting* the right of property.

The principle of improvement as the basis of property rights was working its way into the law, into legal disputes about property, especially over enclosure. It also appeared in political theory, notably in the work of John Locke, who, as we saw in Chapter 5, developed a whole theory of property on that principle. When we unpack his famous idea that individuals acquire a right to property by mixing their labour with it, we find at its heart the notion of improvement, the idea of productivity for profit, the idea that the natural right of property derives from its productive use. People acquire a right to property by giving it value – which Locke makes very clear means exchange value. This had vast implications not only for the domestic practice of enclosure but also for the dispossession of indigenous peoples in colonial territories – and on that score, Locke was quite explicit.

Writing about America and its indigenous peoples, Locke, as we saw, explains that an acre of land in unimproved America may be as naturally fertile as an acre in England, but it is not worth 1/1000 of the English acre, if we calculate 'all the Profit an *Indian* received from it were it valued and sold here'. In other words, the Indian has added no exchange value to the land, which effectively means he has failed to mix his labour with it. The measure of labour is not effort but profitability. We can, then, easily deduce that the Indian has failed to establish his right to the land, which becomes fair game to more 'industrious' and 'rational' colonists. Unimproved land is *waste*, and a man who appropriates it to himself in order to improve it has, by increasing its value, given something to humanity, not taken it away.

Historians of political thought have pointed out that, while Locke was not the first theorist to argue that unoccupied and unused land could be claimed as property by those able and willing to render it fruitful, he introduced an important theoretical innovation by justifying colonial appropriation of unused land without the consent of any local sovereign, providing settlers with a systematic argument that justified their actions on the basis of natural law, without any reference to civil authority.

But Locke's innovation goes much further than this. Even if land is occupied by indigenous peoples, and even if they make use of the land themselves, their land is still open to legitimate colonial expropriation. His notion that property derives from the creation of value, from 'improvement' that enhances exchange value, implies not only that mere occupancy is not enough to establish property rights, or even that hunting-gathering cannot establish the right of property while agriculture can, but also that insufficiently productive and profitable agriculture, by the standards of English agrarian capitalism, effectively constitutes waste. This redefinition of occupancy and waste means that land in America is open to colonization because an acre of land in 'unimproved' America has not produced exchange value comparable to that of improved land in England.

Locke wrote this in the late seventeenth century at a time when agrarian capitalism had already put down deep roots in English society, especially in those parts of the south that he knew best, and when England's colonialism in Ireland and North America already had a well-documented history. Knowing something about that history, domestic and colonial, it is instructive to work backwards from Locke's theory of property. Locke himself had a keen interest not only in the domestic economy but also in the colonies, drafting a constitution for the Carolinas and investing in the slave trade; and his theory of property encompasses the project of 'improvement' both in England and in its colonies, both the domestic experience of agrarian capitalism and the project of colonial settlement, both enclosure at home and expropriation of indigenous land in the colonies, both the interests of Locke's mentor, Lord Shaftesbury, in the productive exploitation of his own estates at home and his involvement in the American colonies.

Keeping all that in mind, we can now look back at the arguments of John Winthrop, first governor of Massachusetts (who had roots in England's Irish settlements and had intended to make his life in Ireland). Justifying the intended plantation of New England in 1629, he makes an argument about the Indians that foreshadows Locke on property in general. The Indians have not been using their lands according to God's will, he insists, 'for the Natives in New England they inclose noe land neither have they any setled habitation nor any tame cattle to improve the land by'. So, as long as the colonists leave them enough for their own (obviously limited) use, the rest can lawfully be taken from them.

But even this is not the first example of an argument like Locke's in the justification of colonial expropriation. There is, for instance, a fascinating document written by one of the principal figures of English imperialism in Ireland in the early seventeenth century, a letter from the lawyer, Sir John Davies, to the Earl of Salisbury, concerning the state of Ireland in 1610. The purpose of the letter is to lay out the legal arguments that were being made by English lawyers (like Davies himself) in justification of the Ulster plantation, the eviction of the Irish, and their replacement by Englishmen and Scots, with some redistribution among the Irish themselves.

First, there is an argument showing that the king has supreme rights over the land not only by English common law but also by Irish customary law (which, of course, has been set aside in any case as no law at all but just 'lewd' and 'unreasonable' custom). Davies then goes on to show that the king is not only entitled by law but also bound in conscience to seize Irish land:

> . . . His Majesty is bound in conscience to use all lawful and just courses to reduce his people from barbarism to civility; the neglect whereof heretofore hath been laid as an imputation upon the

Crown of England. Now civility cannot possibly be planted among them by this mixed plantation of some of the natives and settling of their possessions in a course of Common Law; for if themselves were suffered to possess the whole country, as their septs have done for many hundred of years past, they would never, to the end of the world, build houses, make townships or villages, or manure or improve the land as it ought to be; therefore it stands neither with Christian policy nor conscience to suffer so good and fruitful a country to lie waste like a wilderness, when his Majesty may lawfully dispose it to such persons as will make a civil plantation thereupon.

Again, his majesty may take this course in conscience because it tendeth to the good of the inhabitants many ways; for half their land doth now lie waste, by reason whereof that which is habited is not improved to half the value; but when the undertakers [the settlers] are planted among them . . ., and that land shall be fully stocked and manured, 500 acres will be of better value than 5000 are now.

Eighty years before Locke's *Second Treatise of Government* was published, Sir John Davies is making essentially the same argument for the colonial settlement of Ireland that Locke would later make for the dispossession of American Indians, and the same kind of argument that was made for enclosure in England and the extinction of the customary rights of English commoners. Here, too, the core of the argument is 'improvement', the increase in exchange value derived from improving productivity. Here, too, the issue is not simply occupancy or even fruitful use but relative value. The similarities down to the last detail are truly uncanny: the talk about 'waste', the numerical calculation of the value of improved as against unimproved land, the suggestion that the improving settlers are not taking anything away but *adding* something.

The Irish case is significant not just because it was the earliest but also because Ireland was, in the seventeenth century, a favourite test case or laboratory for English social theory and even natural science. For instance, scientists interested in improving English agriculture thought of Ireland as a perfect location for pilot projects. Some of the most innovative agricultural techniques were tested in Ireland. Ireland was also regarded as the ideal setting for what they called, in the Baconian manner, natural histories of various practices and institutions.

Political and economic thinkers such as William Petty thought of Ireland in those terms. For instance, in 1671–2, he wrote a self-conciously Baconian natural history, *An Essay of Political Anatomy*, on the political anatomy of Ireland, printed in 1691. He tells us that he chose Ireland as his exemplary 'Political Animal' following the model of students of medicine, who 'practice their inquiries upon cheap and common Animals, and such whose actions they are best acquainted with, and where there is the least confusion and perplexure of Parts'. He has known this particular political animal, he says, since it was an embryo. What he means is that he has known Ireland since Cromwell's conquest, when Petty served as his Surveyor General in the conquered territory and, in that capacity, played a leading role in the forcible restructuring of Irish society.

FROM ENCLOSURE TO EMPIRE?

In fact, the English colonial experience, in Ireland and in the Americas, was a major factor in what might be called the self-consciousness of English capitalism itself, making the logic of English domestic property relations more transparent. The understanding of English agrarian capitalism was refracted through that imperial experience. Petty, for instance, who is often called the founder of classical political economy, elaborated the theory of value that is supposed to be his seminal contribution to that field in response to the very concrete practical requirements of his position as Cromwell's Surveyor General, while he was conducting his land survey for the purpose of distributing land among the conquering soldiers.[5]

These ideological developments bring into sharp relief the specific logic of capitalism in the evolution of imperialism. We have seen that from the earliest years of agrarian capitalism in England, its economic logic became not just the driving force of the domestic economy but also an instrument of imperial domination beyond the boundaries of England. We can trace the connections very neatly by following the filiations between the ideology of early capitalism and the ideology of empire. We need not make assumptions about direct influences to see the thread connecting Locke to Winthrop and both to John Davies. There can be little doubt that the English colonial experience, first in Ireland and then in the New World, was a major inspiration in English theories of property and value, the basic tools for understanding their own domestic capitalism – which is nowhere more obvious than in the work of Petty and Locke.

Yet we must push things even further really to see the connections between agrarian capitalism and the new form of imperialism. None of Locke's or Petty's theoretical debts to England's colonial project makes sense unless we also acknowledge that this project had its own practical and theoretical roots in the English domestic economy, in English agrarian capitalism.

The English, again, were not alone in justifying imperial expansion on the grounds that unoccupied land could be claimed by those who would render it fruitful. But they did, as we have seen, introduce important innovations into that argument. It seems to have been in England that it was first suggested – notably by Thomas More, as early as 1516, in his *Utopia* – that the seizure of vacant land could be justified even without the consent of the local sovereign, though it was Locke who gave this principle a systematic theorization.[6] More significantly, the English, particularly Locke, took the argument a major step further by justifying the seizure of land that was indeed occupied, and perhaps even cultivated, on the grounds that the occupants had failed to use the land productively and profitably enough, by the standards of English commercial agriculture. For both John

Davies and John Locke, in their various ways, the critical issue is not simply occupancy but relative value. The Irish farmer or the Indian hunter-gatherer, indeed, the Indian cultivator, may occupy and work the land, but he has failed to add sufficient exchange value to it by means of improvement. In effect, the English had redefined vacancy by redefining *waste*, and the context in which they took that fateful step in imperialist ideology is, again, their own domestic economy.

It is difficult to identify the exact moment in legal history when arguments such as those used to justify colonial expropriation were first made to justify dispossession or enclosure in England itself. But they were already being made in the early seventeenth century; and even before that, debates on enclosure certainly raised questions about productivity and profit. There was certainly a growing 'improvement' literature in the seventeenth century, with roots in the sixteenth, about how to make agriculture more productive, and certainly arguments from improvement later figure in legal disputes over enclosure and other property disputes. There is also no doubt that these early domestic concerns about the productivity and profitability of agriculture, or about the benefits of enclosure in enhancing improvement, lie at the heart of Locke's political theory in the late 1670s and 1680s.

Long before these more formal and systematic theorizations, we can easily detect the agrarian relations, practices, and discourses that generated those later ideologies. The project of bringing the south-east of England to Ireland obviously presupposes the English model on which it was based, and it is hard to imagine the mentality of Sir John Davies without presupposing the mentality of an improving English landlord. It is also impossible to imagine William Petty's theory of value, and its elaboration as an instrument of empire in Ireland, without presupposing the notions of value already firmly implanted in the mind of the improving landlord preoccupied with the profitability of his own estate in England.

Before Petty, and before Sir John Davies, we have the English landlord's surveyor, as we saw in Chapter 5, working out his own rudimentary theory of value. It is not difficult to see the connections between the domestic concerns of these land surveys with Petty's ambitious colonial survey half a century later. Similarly, it is surely no accident that, while Englishmen from John Davies to William Petty were devising schemes for reproducing English agrarian capitalism in Ireland, the French embarked on a scheme to reproduce seigneurialism in New France – just as French landlords and their surveyors would seek to revive their feudal rights at home.

The ideological implications of the English justification of expropriation and colonization on the grounds of 'improvement' were enormous. This kind of imperialism, in which the claims of the imperial power rested on capitalist principles of productive use of property for private profit, was justified on the same basis as individual claims to property. Even if the Irish plantations, for example, started as a project of the royal state, the agents of that project were private 'undertakers', and the colonial project was based on the private actions of industrious settlers, not just the public actions of states and legally constituted political authorities. The imperial legitimacy of the colonial power was rooted in the productive activities of its subjects, its 'improving' settlers. It was becoming difficult to detach the state's jurisdiction over Ireland, or England's imperial claims, from the rights of individual proprietors and their capacity to generate exchange value.

Although the British Empire would be distinctive in the degree to which it relied on white settler colonies, colonization for the private benefit of colonizers was obviously nothing new. Nor was the imperialism of the early modern English the first to depend not only on a powerful imperial state but on a network of private proprietors. After all, the Roman Empire (whose concept of *colonia* the British self-consciously revived) was governed not so much by a massive state apparatus in Rome as by a relatively simple state at home in alliance with local aristocracies throughout the Empire who extracted every material benefit they could from Rome's imperial hegemony. It is true that the English case was distinguished by a distinctive form of appropriation, with a logic of its own. But what was even more distinctive about this form of imperial domination – or rather, what this distinctive form of appropriation implied – was a system with coercions of its own, *economic* imperatives, reinforcing, and eventually capable of replacing, the extra-economic coercion of military conquest and direct political domination. These economic coercions are unique to capitalism.

The ideological implications go even further. The argument for colonial expropriation was not just that improving settlers had the right to expropriate and displace people who were not suitably productive. Nor was it even just that colonizers could, indeed should, expropriate those who might be productive but not producing for commercial profit. The point was that, just as Locke's 'improvers' and enclosers were giving added value to the people they displaced, effectively *creating* value and therefore giving something to the community rather than taking it away, the colonizer, in expropriating local populations, was not robbing subject peoples but adding to the common good.

These colonizers now found their justification in economic rather than extra-economic moral or religious principles, or, more precisely, economic principles took on a moral and religious meaning. Just as human beings engaged in improvement had assumed God's role as creators of value, their project had become the new religion.

8

CAPITALISM AND THE NATION STATE

It is not uncommon to insist on the connections between the emergence of capitalism and the rise of the nation state, or even to define capitalism, at least at its origin, as a system of nation states. Typically, the connections are seen through the prism of one or another theory of 'modernity' or 'rationalization', according to which certain 'modern' or 'rational' economic, political, and cultural forms have developed more or less in tandem, combining a process of urbanization and commercialization with the formation of a 'rational' state.

There are variations on this theme, such as Perry Anderson's suggestion, discussed in Chapter 2, that the emergence of the absolutist state in early modern Europe freed the 'bourgeois' commercial economy from the dead hand of feudalism and landlordly power, separating political and economic spheres by concentrating sovereignty in a centralized state. Immanuel Wallerstein, as we saw, suggests that the European nation state, in sharp contrast to more advanced Asian empires, laid the foundations for capitalism, because the organization of Europe into multiple polities, instead of in one over-arching empire, permitted the development of a trade-based division of labour, without the burden of massive appropriation by an imperial state that syphoned off surpluses that could otherwise have been invested.

But the argument presented in this book requires us to look at the relation between the rise of capitalism and the nation state somewhat differently, building on the premises outlined so far: that capitalism was not simply the natural outcome of certain tranhistorical processes like 'rationalization', technological progress, urbanization, or the expansion of trade; that its emergence required more than the removal of obstacles to increased trade and growing markets or to the exercise of 'bourgeois' rationality; that while certain European, or Western European, conditions, not least the insertion of Europe in a larger and non-European network of international trade, were necessary to its emergence, those same conditions produced diverse effects in various European, and even Western European, cases; and that the necessary conditions for the 'spontaneous' or indigenous and self-sustaining development of a capitalist system, with mutually reinforcing agricultural and industrial sectors, existed only in England.

THE SOVEREIGN TERRITORIAL STATE IN PRE-CAPITALIST EUROPE

The unity of economic and political power that characterized pre-capitalist states, in which exploitation was carried out by 'extra-economic' means – that is, by means of political, judicial, and/or military power, or 'politically constituted property' – has existed in a very wide variety of forms: ancient empires where state power was employed to collect tribute from subject peoples, including their own peasants, and imperial office was the principal means of acquiring great wealth; the 'collective lordships' of commercial city-states in medieval and early modern Europe; the early modern European absolutist state with its 'tax/office' structure, in which public office was a source of private wealth, achieved by extracting taxes especially from peasants; and so on.

The 'modern' nation state emerged out of a very particular pre-capitalist formation: a unity of political and economic power that took the form of a *fragmented* state power, the 'parcellized sovereignty' of Western feudalism, and its distinctive kind of 'extra-economic' power, feudal lordship.[1] The fragmented military, political, and judicial powers of the state became the means by which individual lords extracted surpluses from peasants. At the same time, political parcellization was, as we have seen, matched by economic fragmentation, so that even internal trade, when it extended beyond very local peasant markets, was less like modern capitalist forms of trade in an integrated competitive market than like traditional forms of international commerce, circulating goods between separate markets.

The parcellized sovereignty of feudalism represented a network of very local and personal social relations, which were at once political and economic. This certainly meant that the feudal system was very fragmented. But at the same time, it was in the very nature of these relations that there were no rigid territorial boundaries between one feudal nexus and another. A feudal kingdom, constituted by a series of vertical relations of fealty, bondage, and personal coercive power, and horizontal relations of family and dynastic alliance, was likely to have fairly porous borders, which could be breached or moved by extending or contracting the network of personal bonds and domination. Just as the feudal trading network was not an integrated global system but a series of conveyance and arbitrage operations between one locale and another, feudalism as a social system was an aggregation of personal and local networks with permeable or moveable boundaries. In feudalism, then, the territorial boundaries of political sovereignty tended to be fluid, expanding or contracting with the reach of the lord's, or the monarch's, personal rule, his proprietary domain and family alliances.

The feudal ruling class was eventually compelled to consolidate its fragmented political power in the face of peasant resistance and the plainly untenable disorder of aristocratic conflict. Parcellized sovereignty gave way to more centralized monarchies in some parts of Europe and to the 'modern' nation state. The centralizing monarchies of Europe created territorial states in which the central more or less sovereign power exerted its predominant coercive force over a more or less well-defined territory. But the fluid boundaries of feudalism were never firmly fixed until personal rule was replaced by an impersonal state, and that could never be fully accomplished until the separation of the 'political' and 'economic', the moments of appropriation and coercion, private property and public power. That separation would be completed only in capitalism.

It is certainly true that capitalism developed in the distinctive context of the early modern European state, which was not itself created by capitalism – or, to put it more precisely, capitalism developed in tandem with the process of state formation. But if feudalism was a precondition of capitalism, and if capitalism, with its separation of 'political' and 'economic' spheres, emerged in conjunction with a process of feudal centralization, the process of state formation took different forms in different places, and capitalism was only one of several outcomes of the transition from feudalism. While there were certain common preconditions, not all European, or even Western European, nation states developed in the same way.

One path out of feudalism was absolutism, which had an economic logic quite distinct from capitalist forms of exploitation or capitalist laws of motion. Instead of producing a capitalist economy, it reproduced the pre-capitalist *unity* of political and economic power at the level of the central state, while never completely overcoming the parcellization of feudalism. The most notable example is the absolutist state in France, regarded by many as the prototype of the emerging 'modern' nation state. Formed in a process of state centralization that elevated one among many feudal powers to a position of monarchical dominance, French absolutism remained in many ways rooted in its feudal past.

On the one hand, the bureaucracy that is supposed to be the mark of the French state's modernity represented a structure of offices used by officeholders as a form of private property, a means of appropriating peasant-produced surpluses, what has been called a kind of centralized feudal rent, in the form of taxation.

Property in office even came to be recognized in law as heritable and alienable, like any other private property. This was a mode of appropriation very different, in its means and in its rules for reproduction, from capitalist exploitation – depending on direct coercion to squeeze more surpluses out of the direct producers, instead of on intensifying exploitation by enhancing labour-productivity.

On the other hand, the absolutist state never completely displaced other forms of politically constituted property. It always lived side-by-side, and in tension, with other, more fragmented forms, the remnants of feudal parcellized sovereignty. Aristocrats, the church, and municipalities clung to their old autonomous powers, military, political, or judicial. Even when these powers were fatally weakened by state centralization and no longer represented a fragment of parcellized sovereignty, they often continued to serve as a fiercely protected (occasionally revived or even invented) source of income for their possessors.

At the same time, the central state, competing for the same peasant-produced surpluses, typically co-opted many potential competitors by giving them state office, exchanging one kind of politically constituted property for another. But the remnants of aristocratic privilege and municipal jurisdiction, together with the tensions among various forms of politically constituted property, remained to the end just as much a part of French absolutism as was the centralizing monarchy. Notwithstanding France's 'bourgeois' revolution, we cannot take for granted its 'spontaneous' evolution into capitalism, in the absence of external pressures from an already existing English capitalism.[2]

Elsewhere in Europe, the fragmentation of property and polity were even more marked; and everywhere, these fragmented forms of politically constituted property, like the centralized version, represented a mode of appropriation antithetical to capitalism. They were inimical to capitalism also because they fragmented the economy as well as the state, with their separate local and municipal markets (not to mention internal trade barriers) characterized not by capitalist competition but by the old forms of commercial profit-taking in the sphere of circulation. To put it another way, the parcellization of sovereignty and the parcellization of markets were two sides of the same coin, rooted in the same property relations.

THE STATE IN CAPITALIST ENGLAND

The development of capitalism and the nation state were intertwined in England in a very particular way. England was not, of course, alone in producing a sovereign territorial state, but it was, in the first instance, alone in producing a capitalist system. At the same time, the process that gave rise to English capitalism was accompanied by the development of a more clearly defined territorial sovereignty than in other European nation states. Although capitalism did not give rise to the nation state, and the nation state did not give rise to capitalism, the social transformations that brought about capitalism, with its characteristic separation of economic and political spheres, were the same ones that brought the nation state to maturity.

England never had the same degree of parcellization that existed in the rest of feudal Europe, and the fragmentation of both economy and polity was overcome first and most completely here. Even in the Middle Ages, when England had what appeared to be a thoroughly 'feudal' system of property, in which the law recognized 'no land without its lord', lordship did not carry the same autonomous political power that it had elsewhere, and the monarchy developed in tandem, rather than in competition, with the aristocracy. Of course there were episodes of baronial conflict. But when the monarchy and propertied classes came to blows most dramatically, in the seventeenth-century Civil War, it was not a conflict between different forms of politically constituted property, or even between competing sites of sovereignty, but rather a battle over control of an already centralized sovereign state, because the king was upsetting the balance between the

Crown and Parliament, breaching the traditional alliance summed up in the old formula 'The Crown in Parliament'.

England's particular process of feudal centralization produced a legal and political order more unified than was the European norm. So, for instance, while France, even at the height of its absolutist centralization, still had its regional 'estates', England had long had a unitary national parliament; and when France (even up until the Revolution) had some 360 local law codes, England had a more nationally unified legal system, especially its 'common law' adjudicated by royal courts, which had become the preferred and dominant legal system very early in the development of the English state.

This unity was not simply a matter of political or legal unification. Its corollary was a distinctive degree of economic unification. Already in the seventeenth century, there was something like a national economy, an integrated and increasingly competitive national market centred on London.

Both political and economic unity can be traced to the same source. The centralization of the state in England was not based on a feudal unity of economic and political power. The state did not represent a private resource for officeholders in the way or on the scale that it did in France, nor did the state on the whole have to compete with other forms of politically constituted property. Instead, state formation took the form of a cooperative project, a kind of division of labour between political and economic power, between the monarchical state and the aristocratic ruling class, between a central political power that enjoyed a virtual monopoly of coercive force much earlier than others in Europe and an economic power based on private property in land more concentrated than elsewhere in Europe.

Here, then, was the separation between the moment of coercion and the moment of appropriation, allocated between two distinct but complementary 'spheres', that uniquely characterizes capitalist exploitation. English landlords increasingly depended on purely 'economic' forms of exploitation, while the state maintained order and enforced the whole system of property. Instead of enhancing their own coercive powers to squeeze more out of peasants, landlords relied on the coercive power of the state to sustain the whole system of property, while they exercised their purely economic power, their concentrated land-holdings, to increase the productivity of labour, in conditions where appropriators and producers were both becoming increasingly market-dependent.

The weakness of politically constituted property in England, in other words, meant both the rise of capitalism and the evolution of a truly sovereign and unified national state. It also meant a more sharply defined territorial polity. Just as the separation of the 'political' and the 'economic' in capitalism ended the contestation of sovereignty among competing sites of extra-economic power, so it helped to fix the state's territorial borders by detaching them from the fluctuating fortunes of personal property and dynastic connections.

There were, to sum up, two sides to the historical relation between capitalism and the nation state. On the one hand, that state was not itself produced by capitalism. The 'modern' state, together with 'modern' conceptions of territoriality and sovereignty, emerged out of social relations that had nothing to do with capitalism, in the tensions between parcellized sovereignties and centralizing monarchies.[3] On the other hand, the rise of capitalism, which took place in the context of a rising nation state, brought that state to fruition – or, to put it more precisely, the particular form of English state formation belonged to the same process that brought about capitalism. The transformation of politically constituted property into capitalist property was at the same time, and inseparably, a transformation of the state.

A state with an unambiguous sovereign power over a clearly defined territory did not come completely into its own until capitalist property had displaced pre-capitalist modes of appropriation – that is, until capitalist property displaced both parcellized sovereignty and the fragmented 'economy' associated with politically constituted property. The territorial nation state was part of a more general European process of state formation, but a clearly defined territorial state with a truly sovereign power matured only when political sovereignty became both separate from and allied with a national economy.

CAPITALISM AND INTERNATIONAL RELATIONS

For those who regard capitalism as the consequence of commercial expansion when it reached a critical mass, there is something paradoxical about the development of English capitalism. England was certainly part of a vast trading network. But other European nation states in the early modern period were also deeply involved in the system of international trade, as were non-European civilizations, some of which long had trading networks more highly developed and extensive than the European. What distinguished England – and what was specifically capitalist about it – was not, in the first instance, predominance as a trading nation or any peculiarity in its way of conducting foreign trade. England's peculiarity was not its role in an outwardly expanding commercial system but, on the contrary, its *inward* development, the growth of a unique *domestic* economy.

What marked off England's commercial system from others was a single large and integrated national market, increasingly uniting the country into one economic unit (which eventually embraced the British Isles as a whole), with a specialized division of labour among interdependent regions and a growing, and mutually reinforcing, interaction between agricultural and industrial sectors. While England competed with others in an expanding system of international trade, not least by military means, a new kind of commercial system was emerging at home, which would soon give it an advantage on the international plane too. This system was unique in its dependence on intensive as distinct from extensive expansion, on the extraction of surplus value created in production as distinct from profit in the sphere of circulation, on economic growth based on increasing productivity and competition within a single market – in other words, on capitalism.

Capitalism, then, while it certainly developed within – and could not have developed without – an international system of trade, was a domestic product. But it was not in the nature of capitalism to remain at home for long. Its need for endless accumulation, on which its very survival depended, produced new and distinctive imperatives of expansion. These imperatives operated at various levels. The most obvious was, of course, the imperialist drive. Here again, although other European states were deeply involved in imperialism, capitalism had a transformative effect. The new requirements of capitalism created new imperialist needs, and it was British capitalism that produced an imperialism answering to the specific requirements of capitalist accumulation. Above all, capitalism created new imperialist possibilities by generating *economic* imperatives, the compulsions of the market, which could reach far beyond direct political dominion.

Capitalism also expanded out from Britain in another and more complicated sense. The unique productivity engendered by capitalism, especially in its industrial form, gave Britain new advantages not only in its old commercial rivalries with other European states but also in their military conflicts. So, from the late eighteenth century and especially in the nineteenth, Britain's major European rivals were under pressure to develop their economies in ways that could meet this new challenge. The state itself became a major player. This was true most notably in Germany, with its state-led industrialization, which in the first instance was undoubtedly driven more by older geopolitical and military considerations than by capitalist motivations.[4]

In such cases, the drive for capitalist development did not come from internal property relations like those that had impelled the development of capitalism in England from within. Where, as in France and Germany, there was an adequate concentration of productive forces, capitalism could develop in response to external pressures emanating from an already existing capitalist system elsewhere. States still following a pre-capitalist logic could become effective agents of capitalist development. The point here, however, is not simply that in these later developing capitalisms, as in many others after them, the state played a primary role. What is even more striking is the ways in which the traditional, pre-capitalist state system, together with the old commercial network, became a transmission belt for capitalist imperatives.

The European state system, then, was a conduit for the first outward movement of capitalism. From then on, capitalism spread outward from Europe both by means of imperialism and increasingly by means of economic imperatives. The role of the state in imperial ventures is obvious, but even in the operation of purely economic laws of motion, the state continued to be an unavoidable medium.

Capitalism had emerged first in one country. After that, it could never emerge again in the same way. Every extension of its laws of motion changed the conditions of development thereafter, and every local context shaped the processes of change. But having once begun in a single nation state, and having been followed by other nationally organized processes of economic development, capitalism has spread not by erasing national boundaries but by reproducing its national organization, creating an increasing number of national economies and nation states. The inevitably uneven development of separate, if interrelated, national entities, especially when subject to imperatives of competition, has virtually guaranteed the persistence of national forms.

CAPITALISM AND THE NATION STATE

Although the world today is more than ever before a world of nation states, we are constantly being told that the global expansion of capitalism has ruptured its historic association with the nation state. The state, we are assured, is being pushed aside by 'globalization' and transnational forces.

But, while no one would deny the global reach of capital, there is little evidence that today's 'global' capital is less in need of national states than were earlier capitalist interests. Global capital, no less than 'national' capital, relies on nation states to maintain local conditions favourable to accumulation as well as to help it navigate the global economy. It might, then, be more accurate to say that 'globalization' is characterized less by the decline of the nation state than by a growing contradiction between the global scope of capital and its persistent need for more local and national forms of 'extra-economic' support, a growing disparity between its economic reach and its political grasp.

We can make sense of this contradiction by looking more closely at the historic separation between the 'economic' and the 'political' in capitalism, in contrast to earlier forms. The pre-capitalist unity of economic and political powers, such as that of feudal lordship, meant, among other things, that the economic powers of the feudal lord could never extend beyond the reach of his personal ties or alliances and extra-economic powers, his military force, political rule, or judicial authority. Nor, for that matter, could the economic powers of the absolutist state or any pre-capitalist empire exceed its extra-economic range.

Unlike other systems of exploitation, in which appropriating classes or states extract surplus labour from producers by direct coercion, capitalist exploitation is characterized by a division of labour between the 'economic' moment of appropriation and the 'extra-economic' or 'political' moment of coercion. Underlying this separation is the market dependence of all economic actors, appropriators and producers, which generates economic impera-tives distinct and apart from direct political coercion. This sepa-ration – which creates two distinct 'spheres', each with its own dynamics, its own temporalities, and its own spatial range – is both a source of strength and a source of contradiction.

On the one hand, the distinctive division of labour between the economic and political moments of capitalism, and between economic imperatives and political coercion, makes possible capitalism's unique capacity for universalization and spatial expansion. Capital is not only uniquely *driven* to extend its economic reach but also uniquely *able* to do so. The self-expansion of capital is not limited to what the capitalist can squeeze out of the direct producers by direct coercion, nor is capital accumulation confined within the spatial range of personal domination. By means of specifically economic (market) imperatives, capital is uniquely able to escape the limits of direct coercion and move far beyond the borders of political authority. This makes possible both its distinctive forms of class domination and its particular forms of imperialism.

On the other hand, while the scope of capitalist economic imperatives can far outreach direct political rule and legal authority, the same disjunction that makes this possible is the root of an irreducible contradiction. The economic imperatives of capitalism are always in need of support by extra-economic powers of regulation and coercion, to create and sustain the conditions of accumulation and maintain the system of capitalist property. The transfer of certain 'political' powers to capital can never eliminate the need to retain others in a formally separate political 'sphere', preserving the division between the moment of economic appropriation and the moment of political coercion. Nor can purely economic imperatives ever completely supplant direct political coercion, or, indeed, survive at all without political support.

In fact, capitalism, in some ways more than any other social form, needs politically organized and legally defined stability, regularity, and predictability in its social arrangements. Yet these are conditions of capital's existence and self-reproduction that it cannot provide for itself and that its own inherently anarchic laws of motion constantly subvert. To stabilize its constitutive social relations – between capital and labour or capital and other capitals – capitalism is especially reliant on legally defined and politically authorized regularities. Business transactions at every level require consistency and reliable enforcement, in contractual relations, monetary standards, exchanges of property. The coercions that sustain these regularities must exist apart from capital's own powers of appropriation if it is to preserve its capacity for self-expansion.

Capitalist transactions also require an elaborate infrastructure that its own profit-maximizing imperatives are ill equipped to provide. And finally, in a system of market dependence, access to the means of subsistence is subject to the vagaries of the market, especially for the propertyless majority, whose access even to the means of labour depends on selling their labour-power. A system like this, where the economy has been 'disembedded' from other social relations, will also have a distinctive need for politically organized social provision, even just to keep people alive through times when they cannot sell their labour-power, and to ensure a 'reserve army' of workers.

This means that capitalism remains dependent on extra-economic conditions, political and legal supports. Until now, no one has found a more effective means of supplying those supports than the political form with which capitalism has been historically, if not causally, connected: the old nation state. As much as 'global' capital might like a corresponding 'global' state, the kind of day-to-day stability, regularity, and predictability required for capital accumulation is inconceivable on anything like a global scale.

To be sure, there does exist a military power whose scope is as close to global as the world has ever seen. As this edition goes to press, the world is seeing yet another display of that coercive power. Yet however successful the constant threat of US military power may be in enforcing the 'global' economy, the nature and capabilities of such a military power are completely at odds with capital's daily needs. High-tech bombing, however 'smart', is hardly designed to create the stable and predictable social order, or the complex infrastructure, required by capital in its daily affairs.

The economic imperatives of capitalism could be said to have created a global order more integrated than ever before, maybe even a form of integration that for the first time constitutes what some would call a global *society*. But the social system that binds together a vast and varied array of social networks and national economies is of a very peculiar kind. There is nothing else in the history of humanity to compare with the kind of social system created by capitalism: a complex network of tight interdependence among large numbers of people, and social classes, not joined by personal ties or direct political domination but connected by their market dependence and the market's imperative network of social relations and processes. This impersonal social system is uniquely capable of extending far beyond the reach of personal ties and direct domination. But to sustain this vast impersonal network requires close social and legal controls, such as those provided by the nation state. It is hard to imagine a 'global' society, based on capitalist economic relations, that could be sustained without a multitude of much more local powers of coercion and administration.

At any rate, the development of a rudimentary global society is, and is likely to remain, far behind the contrary effect of capitalist integration: the formation of many unevenly developed economies with varied and self-enclosed social systems, presided over by many nation states. The national economies of advanced capitalist societies will continue to compete with one another, while 'global' capital (always based in one or another national entity) will continue to profit from uneven development, the differentiation of social conditions among national economies, and the preservation of exploitable low-cost labour regimes, which have created the widening gap between rich and poor so characteristic of 'globalization'.

So the capitalist economy has an irreducible need for 'extra-economic' supports whose spatial range can never match its economic reach. In the earliest days of capitalism, when England's domestic economy more or less coincided with its national political regime, there was no obvious disjunction between the economic reach of capital and the political/jurisdictional reach of the nation state. But both England's national dominion and its domestic economy began to extend their reach very early in the development of the English nation state and English capitalism. The multinational character of the British Isles was already a major factor in the formation of the Tudor state, and England also sought ways of extending the reach of its economic imperatives beyond the capacities of its political and military dominion, already in its early forms of colonialism. The history of capitalist development since then, which has seen a proliferation of nation states, has also been marked by a growing distance between the economic reach of capital and the political dominion of any single nation state.

That increasing disparity between the global economy and the territorial nation state in no way signals the end of capitalism's need, however contradictory, for a spatially fragmented political and legal order. On the contrary, that contradiction results from the persistence of that need; and for the foreseeable future, it is most likely to be met by something like the nation state. The strongest challenges to existing nation states, to their boundaries or indeed to their very existence, are more likely to come from oppositional forces of various kinds than from the agents of capital or the impersonal forces of the market.

At the same time, as long as global capital continues to depend on the support of local states, both in the imperial powers and in subordinate economies, the state will be an essential terrain of opposition, and the growing distance between global capital and its political supports will open up new spaces for resistance.

9

MODERNITY AND POSTMODERNITY

The naturalization of capitalism implicit in the conventional identification of *bourgeois* with *capitalist* and both with *modernity*, which still persists even in today's most iconoclastic theories, has the effect of disguising the specificity of capitalism, if not conceptualizing it away altogether. Now let us turn briefly to the other side of the coin. The point is not just that capitalism is historically specific. If some essential aspects of 'modernity' have little to do with capitalism, then the identification of capitalism with modernity may disguise the specificity of a *non*-capitalist modernity, too.

MODERNITY VERSUS CAPITALISM: FRANCE AND ENGLAND

Whatever else people mean by 'modernity', and whether they think it is good or bad or both, they usually believe it has something to do with what sociologist Max Weber called the process of *rationalization*: the rationalization of the state in bureaucratic organization, the rationalization of the economy in industrial capitalism, the rationalization of culture in the spread of education, the decline of superstition, and the progress of science and technology. The process of rationalization is typically associated with certain intellectual or cultural patterns that go back to the Enlightenment: rationalism and an obsession with rational planning, a fondness for 'totalizing' views of the world, the standardization of knowledge, universalism (a belief in universal truths and values), and a belief in linear progress, especially of reason and freedom.

The Enlightenment is typically conceived of as a, if not the, major turning point in the advance of modernity, and the conflation of modernity with capitalism is most readily visible in the way theories of modernity connect the Enlightenment with capitalism. The characteristic features of the Enlightenment are supposed to be associated with the development of capitalism, either because early capitalism, in the process of unfolding itself, created them, or because the advancement of 'rationalization' that produced the Enlightenment also brought capitalism with it. Weber, for instance, is famous for distinguishing among various meanings of rationality (formal or instrumental versus substantive, and so on), yet his argument about the historical process of rationalization depends, of course, on *assimilating* the various meanings of reason and rationality, so that the instrumental rationality of capitalism is by definition related to reason in its Enlightenment meaning. For better or worse, the process that brought us the best of Enlightenment principles – a resistance to all arbitrary power, a commitment to universal human emancipa-tion, and a critical stance toward all kinds of authority, whether intellectual, religious, or political – is, according to this view, the same process that brought us the capitalist organization of production.

To unravel the conflation of capitalism and modernity, we might begin by situating the Enlightenment in its own historical setting. Much of the Enlightenment project belongs to a distinctly *non*-capitalist – not just *pre*-capitalist – society. Many features of the Enlightenment, in other words, are rooted in non-capitalist social property relations. They belong to a social form that is not just a transitional point on the way to capitalism but an alternative route out of feudalism. In particular, the French Enlightenment belongs to the absolutist state in France.

The absolutist state in eighteenth-century France functioned not just as a political form but as an economic resource for a substantial section of the ruling class. In that sense, it represents not just the political but also the economic or material context of the Enlightenment. The absolutist state was a centralized instrument of extra-economic surplus extraction, and office in the state was a form of property that gave its possessors access to peasant-produced surpluses. There also were other, decentralized forms of extra-economic appropriation, the residues of feudalism and its so-called 'parcellized sovereignties'. These forms of extra-economic appropriation were, in other words, directly antithetical to the purely *economic* form of *capitalist* exploitation.

Now consider the fact that the principal home of the so-called 'project of modernity', eighteenth-century France, was an overwhelmingly rural society, with a limited and fragmented internal market. Its markets still operated on non-capitalist principles: not the appropriation of surplus value from commodified labour-power, not the creation of value in production, but the age-old practices of commercial profit-taking – profit on alienation, buying cheap and selling dear, with great commercial wealth derived especially from trading in luxury goods or supplies for the state. The overwhelmingly peasant population was the antithesis of a mass consumer market. As for the bourgeoisie, which is supposed to be the main material source, so to speak, of the Enlightenment, it was *not* a capitalist class. In fact, it was not, for the most part, even a traditional commercial class. The main bourgeois actors in the Enlightenment, and later in the French Revolution, were professionals, officeholders, and intellectuals. Their quarrel with the aristocracy had little to do with liberating capitalism from the fetters of feudalism.

Where, then, did the principles of so-called 'modernity' come from? Did they come out of a new but growing capitalism? Did they represent an aspiring capitalist class struggling against a feudal aristocracy? Can we at least say that capitalism was the unintended consequence of the project of bourgeois modernity? Or did that project represent something different?

Consider the class interests of the French bourgeoisie. One way of focusing on them is to turn to the French Revolution, often treated as the culmination of the Enlightenment project. What were the main revolutionary objectives of the bourgeoisie? At the core of its programme were civil equality, the attack on privilege, and a demand for 'careers open to talent'. This meant, for example, equal access to the highest state offices, which tended to be monopolized by birth and wealth and which the aristocracy were threatening to close off altogether. It also meant a more equitable system of taxation, so that the burden would no longer be disproportionately carried by the Third Estate for the benefit of the privileged estates, among whose most cherished privileges were exemptions from taxation. The targets of these complaints were the aristocracy and the church.

How did these bourgeois interests express themselves ideologically? Take the example of universalism, the belief in certain principles that apply to humanity in general at all times and places. Universalism has had a long history in the West, but it had a very special meaning and salience for the French bourgeoisie. To put it briefly, the bourgeois challenge to privilege and the privileged estates, to the nobility and the church, expressed itself in asserting universalism against aristocratic particularism. The bourgeoisie challenged the aristocracy by invoking the universal principles of citizenship, civic equality, and the 'nation' – a universalistic identity that transcended the more particular and exclusive identities of kinship, tribe, village, status, estate, or class.

In other words, *universality* was opposed to *privilege* in its literal meaning as a special or private law. Universality stood against privilege and differential rights. It was a fairly easy step from attacking traditional privilege to attacking the principles of custom and tradition in general. And this kind of challenge easily became a theory of history, in which the bourgeoisie and its organic intellectuals were assigned a leading role as the historic agents of a rupture with the past, the embodiments of reason and freedom, the vanguard of progress.

As for the bourgeois attitude toward the absolutist state, it is rather more ambiguous. As long as the bourgeoisie had reasonable access to lucrative state careers, the monarchical state suited it well; and even later, the so-called 'bourgeois revolution' completed the centralizing project of absolutism. In fact, in some ways the bourgeois challenge to the traditional order, far from repudiating absolutist principles, simply extended them.

Take, again, the principle of universality. The monarchical state even in the sixteenth century had challenged the feudal claims of the nobility – often with the support of the Third Estate and the bourgeoisie in particular – by claiming to represent universality against the particularity of the nobility and other competing jurisdictions. The bourgeoisie also inherited and extended other absolutist principles: the preoccupation with rational planning and standardization, for example, pioneered by the absolutist state and its leading officials, like Richelieu and Colbert. After all, even the standardization of the French language was part of the absolutist state's centralizing project, a project of 'rationalization' that had its classic cultural expression in the formal gardens at Versailles.[1]

Scholars like Marshall Berman and David Harvey, who have given us some of the most important treatments of modernity (and postmodernity), often emphasize the duality of the modern consciousness, which goes back to the Enlightenment. That dualistic sensibility, they say, combines universality and immutability with a sensitivity to ephemerality, contingency, fragmentation. The argument seems to be that the preoccupation with universality and absolute truth was from the start an attempt to make sense out of the fleeting, ephemeral, and constantly mobile and changing experience of modern life, which they associate with capitalism.

Berman quotes some passages from Rousseau's novel *Julie, ou*

La Nouvelle Eloise (1761), as one of the earliest expressions of that sensibility (he calls Rousseau 'the archetypal modern voice in the early phase of modernity').[2] The most telling passage comes from a letter in which Rousseau's character St Preux records his reactions on coming to Paris. What Berman sees here is the modernist sense of new possibilities, combined with the unease and uncertainty that comes from constant motion, change, and diversity. It is an experience that Berman associates with an early phase of capitalism.

But we can perhaps see something rather different in the words of St Preux, or even in Berman's own account of the 'maelstrom' of modern life. We can see not so much the experience of modern *capitalism* as the age-old fear and fascination aroused by the *city*. So much of what Rousseau's St Preux, and Marshall Berman himself, have to say about the experience of 'modern life' could have been said by the Italian countrydweller arriving in the ancient city of Rome. It may be no accident that the literary tropes associated with this 'experience of modernity' – Rousseau's and those of other European writers – typically come not from a highly urbanized society but from societies with a still overwhelmingly rural population.

At any rate, the ideology of the French bourgeoisie in the eighteenth century had not much to do with capitalism and much more to do with struggles over *non*-capitalist forms of appropriation, conflicts over extra-economic powers of exploitation. There is no need to reduce the Enlightenment to crude class ideology. After all, among some of the greatest Enlightenment figures were aristocrats – like Condorcet. The point is rather that in this particular historical conjuncture, in distinctly non-capitalist conditions, even bourgeois class ideology took the form of a larger vision of general human emancipation, not just emancipation for the bourgeoisie. For all its limitations, this was an emancipatory universalism – which is, of course, why it could be taken up by much more democratic and revolutionary forces.

To see the complexities here, we need only compare France

with England. To reiterate, England in the eighteenth century at the height of agrarian capitalism had a growing urban population, which formed a much larger proportion of the total population than in France. Small proprietors were being dispossessed, not just by direct coercion but also by economic pressures. London was the largest city in Europe. There was a far more integrated – and competitive – internal market, the first national market in the world. There already existed the beginning of a mass consumer market for cheap everyday goods, especially food and textiles, and an increasingly proletarianized workforce. England's productive base in agriculture was already operating on essentially capitalist principles, with an aristocracy deeply involved in agrarian capitalism and new forms of commerce. And England was in the process of creating an industrial capitalism.

What were the characteristic cultural and ideological expressions of English capitalism in the same period?[3] Not Cartesian rationalism and rational planning but the 'invisible hand' of classical political economy and the philosophy of British empiricism. Not the formal garden of Versailles but the irregular, apparently unplanned, 'natural' landscape garden. Even the English state that promoted the early rise of capitalism was far less 'rational' in Weberian terms than was the bureaucratic state of the French *ancien régime*; and the English legal system based on the common law is to this day less 'rational' than the Napoleonic code that followed the French Revolution, or other continental systems based on Roman law.

This is not, of course, to say that the English played no part in the more general European Enlightenment. It hardly needs saying, for instance, that English thinkers made important contributions to the critical temper of the Enlightenment. And there certainly was, in England, an interest in science and technology shared with its European neighbors. Nor should it need saying that the French Enlightenment itself owed much to Bacon, Locke, and Newton. But the characteristic ideology that set England apart from other European cultures was above all the ideology of 'improvement': not the Enlightenment idea of the improvement of *humanity* but the improvement of *property*, the ethic – and indeed the science – of profit, the commitment to increasing the productivity of labour, the production of exchange value, and the practice of enclosure and dispossession.

This ideology, especially the notion of agricultural improvement and the associated improvement literature produced in England, was conspicuously absent in eighteenth-century France, where peasants dominated production and landlords retained their rentier mentality – as, for that matter, did the bourgeoisie on the whole. (The exception, by the way, proves the rule: the Physiocrats, those French political economists for whom English agriculture was a model to emulate.[4])

Now if we want to look for the roots of a *destructive* 'modernity' – the ideology, say, of technocentrism and ecological degradation – we might start by looking in the project of 'improvement', the subordination of all human values to productivity and profit, rather than in the Enlightenment. Might we say that it is no accident that the mad cow disease scandal happened in Britain, the birthplace of 'improvement', or that, more recently, Britain has seen the most massive outbreak of foot-and-mouth disease, widely attributed to intensive farming and marketing practices?

POSTMODERNITY

Attacking the so-called 'Enlightenment project' has by now become an unthinking cliché. The Enlightenment values enumerated earlier are supposed to be – and this is one of the milder indictments – 'at the root of the disasters that have racked humanity throughout [the twentieth] century', everything from world wars and imperialism to ecological destruction.[5] This is not the place to pursue all the latest absurdities, by now far exceeding the reasonable insights that may once have been contained in critiques of the Enlightenment, with their acknowledgement of its duality, both the goods and the evils that have issued from its principles of reason and progress. The important point is that we are being invited to jettison all that is best in the Enlightenment project – especially its commitment to a universal human emancipation – and to blame these values for destructive effects we should be ascribing to capitalism. There are, then, many reasons, intellectual and political, for separating out the Enlightenment project from those aspects of our current condition that overwhelmingly belong not to the 'project of modernity' but to capitalism.

As commonly used, the concept of modernity dissolves some essential distinctions between social and cultural forms that do belong to capitalism and those that do not. In its tendency to conflate *bourgeois* with *capitalist*, it belongs to the standard view of history that takes capitalism for granted as the outcome of already existing tendencies, even natural laws, when and where they are given a chance. In the evolutionary process leading from early forms of exchange to modern industrial capitalism, modernity kicks in when these shackled economic forces and bourgeois economic rationality are liberated from traditional constraints. And so, *modernity* equals *bourgeois society* equals *capitalism*.

This concept of modernity has recently been supplemented with the idea of *post*modernity. The postmodern epoch has been variously described, but always, of course, in relation to modernity. Postmodernity generally represents a phase of capitalism marked by certain distinctive economic and technological characteristics (the 'information age', 'lean production', 'flexible accumulation', 'disorganized capitalism,' consumerism, and so on). But, more particularly, it is marked by certain cultural formations summed up in the formula 'postmodern*ism*', whose single most outstanding feature is its challenge to the 'Enlightenment project'.

Postmodernism is said to have replaced the culture of modernism and the intellectual patterns associated with the 'project of modernity'. The project of modernity, according to these accounts, seems to have begun in the eighteenth century, or at least its defining moment was the Enlightenment, though it came to fruition in the nineteenth century. The so-called 'Enlightenment project' is, again, supposed to represent rationalism, technocentrism, the standardization of knowledge and production, a belief in linear progress, and in universal, absolute truths. *Post-modernism* is understood as a reaction to that project – though it can also be seen as rooted in 'modernism', in the scepticism and the emphasis on uncertainty, change, and contingency associated with 'modernist' cultural forms in the twentieth century but which were, some would argue, already present in the Enlightenment. Postmodernism sees the world as essentially fragmented and indeterminate, rejects any 'totalizing' discourses, any 'metanarratives', any comprehensive and universalistic theories about the world and history. It also rejects any universalistic political projects, even universalistic emancipatory projects – in other words, projects for a general *human* emancipation rather than very particular struggles against very diverse and particular oppressions.

Some theories of postmodernity have been very illuminating, telling us much about contemporary capitalism and especially about its cultural forms.[6] But the concept itself is, in essence, an inversion of 'modernity' in its conventional meaning and carries with it many of the same problematic presuppositions. This modernity belongs to a view of history that *cuts across* the great divide between capitalist and non-capitalist societies, a view that treats specifically capitalist laws of motion as if they were the universal laws of history and lumps together various very different historical developments, capitalist and non-capitalist. The idea of postmodernity is derived from a conception of modernity that, at its worst, makes capitalism historically invisible or, at the very least, naturalizes it.

It is important to notice, too, that even the *critique* of modernity can have the same effect of naturalizing capitalism. This effect was already visible long before today's postmodernist fashions, for instance in the sociological theories of Weber, specifically his theory of rationalization. The process of rationalization – the progress of reason and freedom associated with the Enlightenment – had, according to Weber, liberated humanity from traditional constraints. But at the same time, rationalization had produced and disguised a new oppression, the 'iron cage' of modern organizational forms.

There is, of course, much to be said for acknowledging the two sides of 'modernity', not only the advances it is said to represent but also the destructive possibilities inherent in its productive capacities, its technologies, and its organizational forms – even in its universalistic values. But in an argument like Weber's, there is something more. Capitalism, like bureaucratic domination, is just a natural extension of the long-term progress of reason and freedom. It is worth noting, too, that in Weber we find something closely akin to the postmodernist ambivalence toward capitalism, in which lament is never very far away from celebration.

So postmodernity follows a modernity in which *bourgeois* is identical with *capitalist*, and Enlightenment rationalism is indistinguishable from the economic rationality of capitalism. These equations unavoidably entail some familiar assumptions about the origin of capitalism, especially that capitalism is already present in bourgeois rationality, just waiting for the moment of release. The idea of postmodernity certainly focuses our attention on historical transformations *within* capitalism, but it does so by disguising the transformations *between* capitalist and non-capitalist societies. The specificity of capitalism is again lost in the continuities of history, and the capitalist system is naturalized in the inevitable progress of the eternally rising bourgeoisie.

CONCLUSION

This book has been about the origin of capitalism. What does that origin tell us about the nature of the system itself?

First, it reminds us that capitalism is not a natural and inevitable consequence of human nature, or of the age-old social tendency to 'truck, barter, and exchange'. It is a late and localized product of very specific historical conditions. The expansionary drive of capitalism, reaching a point of virtual universality today, is not the consequence of its conformity to human nature or to some transhistorical law, or of some racial or cultural superiority of 'the West', but the product of its own historically specific internal laws of motion, its unique capacity as well as its unique need for constant self-expansion. Those laws of motion required vast social transformations and upheavals to set them in train. They required a transformation in the human metabolism with nature, in the provision of life's basic necessities.

Second, capitalism has, from the beginning, been a deeply contradictory force. The very least that can be said is that the capitalist system's unique capacity, and need, for self-sustaining growth has never been incompatible with regular stagnation and economic downturns. On the contrary, the very same logic that drives the system forward makes it inevitably susceptible to economic instabilities, which require constant 'extra-economic' interventions, if not to control them then at least to compensate for their destructive effects.

But the system's contradictions have always gone far beyond the vagaries of economic cycles. We need only consider the most obvious effects of English agrarian capitalism: the conditions for material prosperity existed in early modern England in historically unprecedented ways, yet those conditions were achieved at the cost of widespread dispossession and intense exploitation. These new conditions also established the foundation and seeds for new and more effective forms of colonial expansion and imperialism in search of new markets, labour forces, and resources.

Then there are the corollaries of 'improvement': productivity and the ability to feed a vast population set against the subordination of all other considerations to the imperatives of profit. This means, among other things, that people who could be fed are often left to starve. There is, in general, a great disparity between the productive capacities of capitalism and the quality of life it delivers. The ethic of 'improvement' in its original sense, in which production is inseparable from profit, is also the ethic of exploitation, poverty, and homelessness.

Irresponsible land use and environmental destruction are also consequences of the ethic of productivity for profit – as we have seen most dramatically in recent agricultural scandals. Capitalism was born at the very core of human life, in the interaction with nature on which life itself depends, and the transformation of that interaction by agrarian capitalism revealed the inherently destructive impulses of a system in which the very fundamentals of existence are subjected to the requirements of profit. In other words, the origin of capitalism revealed the essential secret of capitalism.

The expansion of capitalist imperatives throughout the world has regularly reproduced effects that it had at the beginning within its country of origin: dispossession, extinction of customary property rights, the imposition of market imperatives, and environmental destruction. These processes have extended their reach from the relations between exploiting and exploited classes to the relations between imperialist and subordinate countries.

But if the destructive effects of capitalism have constantly reproduced themselves, its positive effects have not been nearly as consistent since the system's moment of origin. Once capitalism was established in one country, once it began to impose its imperatives on the rest of Europe and ultimately the whole world, its development in other places could never follow the same course as it had in its place of origin. The existence of one capitalist society thereafter transformed all others, and the subsequent expansion of capitalist imperatives constantly changed the conditions of economic development.

There is also a more general lesson to be drawn from the experience of English agrarian capitalism. Once market imperatives set the terms of social reproduction, all economic actors – both appropriators and producers, even if they remain in possession, or indeed outright ownership, of the means of production – are subject to the demands of competition, increasing productivity, capital accumulation, and the intense exploitation of labour.

For that matter, even the absence of a division between appropriators and producers is no guarantee of immunity. Once the market is established as an economic 'discipline' or 'regulator', once economic actors become market-dependent for the conditions of their own reproduction, even workers who own the means of production, individually or collectively, will be obliged to respond to the market's imperatives – to compete and accumulate, to let 'uncompetitive' enterprises and their workers go to the wall, and to exploit themselves. The history of agrarian capitalism, and everything that followed from it, should make it clear that wherever market imperatives regulate the economy and govern social reproduction, there will be no escape from exploitation. There can, in other words, be no such thing as a truly 'social' or democratic market, let alone a 'market socialism'.

I vividly remember – though the historic days of the Communist collapse now seem very distant – how idealistic democrats in the former Soviet Union and Eastern Europe responded to warnings about the market from the Western left (at a time when there still seemed to be an anti-market left in the West, and still some chance of dialogue between that left and more progressive forces in the former Communist countries). When people warned that the market means not only supermarkets with vast quantities and varieties of consumer goods but also unemployment, poverty, environmental destruction, the degradation of public services and culture, the reply would be, 'Yes, of course, but that's not what we mean by the market.' The idea was that you could pick and choose what you want from the self-regulating market. The market can act as a regulator of the economy just enough to guarantee some rationality, some correspondence between what people want and what is produced. The market can act as a signal, a source of information, a form of communication between consumers and producers, and it can guarantee that useless or inefficient enterprises will shape up or be winnowed out. But we can dispense with its nastier side.

All this no doubt seems as naïve to many Russians and Eastern Europeans now as it did to some Western Marxists then, but the irony is that many on the Western left today are inclined to think that the market as an economic regulator is amenable to choice between its beneficent disciplines and its more destructive consequences. It is difficult to explain in any other way the notion of 'market socialism', that contradiction in terms, or even the less utopian conception of the 'social market', in which the market's ravages can be controlled by state regulation and an enhancement of social rights.

This is not to say that a social market would be no better than unchecked free market capitalism. Nor does it mean that some institutions and practices associated with the market could not be adapted to a socialist economy. But we cannot refuse to confront the implications of the one irreducible condition without which the market cannot act as an economic discipline: the market dependence of direct producers, and specifically its most extreme form, the commodification of labour-power – a condition that places the strictest limits on the 'socialization' of the market and its capacity to assume a human face.[1]

No one would deny that capitalism has brought with it historically unprecedented material advances. But today it is more obvious than ever that the imperatives of the market will not allow capital to prosper without depressing the conditions of great multitudes of people and degrading the environment throughout the world. We have now reached the point where the destructive effects of capitalism are outstripping its material gains. No 'developing' economy setting out on the capitalist road today, for example, is likely to achieve even the contradictory development that England underwent. With the pressures of competition, accumulation, and exploitation imposed by more developed capitalist economies, and with the inevitable crises of overcapacity engendered by capitalist competition, the attempt to achieve material prosperity according to capitalist principles is increasingly likely to bring with it the negative side of the capitalist contradiction, its dispossession and destruction, more than its material benefits – certainly for the vast majority.

There is, if anything, a growing disparity between the material capacities created by capitalism and the quality of life it can deliver. This is visible not only in the growing gap between rich and poor but also, for instance, in the deterioration of public services in the very countries – such as the US and UK – where the principles of the capitalist market are most uninhibited. It is true that parts of Continental Europe enjoy better public services, to say nothing of their often more congenial urban environments. But these advantages (which are, in any case, at growing risk) owe far more to the legacy of absolutism or to pre-capitalist burgher cultures than to the logic of capitalism.[2]

Capitalism is also incapable of promoting sustainable development, not because it encourages technological advances that are capable of straining the earth's resources but because the purpose of capitalist production is exchange value not use value, profit not people. This produces, on the one hand, massive waste and, on the other, inadequate provision of basic necessities, such as affordable housing. Capitalism can certainly produce and even profit from energy-efficient technologies, but its own inherent logic systematically prohibits their sustainable utilization. Just as the requirements of profit and capital accumulation inevitably drive production beyond consumption and beyond the limits of use, they also compel destruction long before the possibilities of use are exhausted. Whatever capitalism may do to enable the efficient use of resources, its own imperatives will always drive it further. Without constantly breaching the limits of conservation, without constantly moving forward the boundaries of waste and destruction, there can be no capital accumulation.

As capitalism spreads more widely and penetrates more deeply into every aspect of social life and the natural environment, its contradictions are increasingly escaping all our efforts to control them. The hope of achieving a humane, truly democratic, and ecologically sustainable capitalism is becoming transparently unrealistic. But although that alternative is unavailable, there remains the real alternative of socialism.

NOTES

INTRODUCTION

1. In *The Pristine Culture of Capitalism: A Historical Essay on Old Regimes and Modern States* (London: Verso, 1991), I called this model of history the 'bourgeois paradigm'.

1. THE COMMERCIALIZATION MODEL AND ITS LEGACY

1. Henri Pirenne's most famous work was *Mohammed and Charlemagne* (London: Allen and Unwin, 1956), but a general summary of his whole thesis is presented in a series of his lectures, *Medieval Cities: The Origins and the Revival of Trade* (Princeton: Princeton University Press, 1969).
2. For more on how Weber adheres to the commercialization model, see my *Democracy Against Capitalism: Renewing Historical Materialism* (Cambridge: Cambridge University Press, 1995), chap. 5.
3. Robert Brenner makes this point in 'Agrarian Class Structure and Economic Development in Pre-Industrial Europe', in T. H. Aston and C. H. E. Philpin, eds, *The Brenner Debate: Agrarian Class Structure and Economic Development in Pre-Industrial Europe* (Cambridge: Cambridge University Press, 1985), p. 10.
4. See, above all, Immanuel Wallerstein, *The Modern World System*, 3 vols (New York: Academic Press, 1974–88).
5. Perry Anderson, 'Maurice Thomson's War', *London Review of Books*, 4 November 1993, p. 17.

6. Among the most prominent 'revisionist' historians of England are Conrad Russell and John Morrill.

7. Michael Mann, *The Sources of Social Power*, Vol. I (Cambridge: Cambridge University Press, 1986), p. 373.

8. Ibid., p. 374.

9. Karl Polanyi, *The Great Transformation* (Boston: Beacon Press, 1957), and George Dalton, ed., *Primitive, Archaic, and Modern Economies: Essays of Karl Polanyi* (Boston: Beacon Press, 1971).

10. Polanyi, *Great Transformation*, p. 76.

11. Ibid., p. 42.

12. Ibid., p. 41.

13. Ibid., p. 40.

14. Ibid., p. 33.

15. Ibid., p. 37.

16. Ibid.

17. Daniel R. Fusfield, 'The Market in History', *Monthly Review* 45 (May 1993), p. 6.

18. This discussion draws on my article 'Eurocentric Anti-Eurocentrism', *Against the Current* 92 (May/June 2001), pp. 29–35.

2. MARXIST DEBATES

1. On the two theories of history in Marx, see George Comninel, *Rethinking the French Revolution: Marxism and the Revisionist Challenge* (London: Verso, 1987). See also Robert Brenner, 'Bourgeois Revolution and Transition to Capitalism', in A. L. Beier, David Cannadine, and James M. Rosenheim, eds, *The First Modern Society* (Cambridge: Cambridge University Press, 1989).

2. R. H. Hilton, ed., *The Transition from Feudalism to Capitalism* (London: Verso, 1976).

3. Maurice Dobb in ibid., p. 59.

4. Hilton in ibid., p. 27.

5. Paul Sweezy in ibid., p. 49.

6. Ibid., p. 54.

7. Ibid., pp. 106–7.

8. Ibid., p. 46.

9. Brenner, 'The Origins of Capitalist Development: A Critique of Neo-Smithian Marxism', *New Left Review* 104 (July/August 1977), pp. 25–92.

10. See, for example, Hilton, 'Capitalism – What's in a Name?' in Hilton, ed., *Transition*, pp. 157–9.

11. Perry Anderson, *Lineages of the Absolutist State* (London: Verso, 1974), p. 19.

12. Ibid.

13. Ibid., p. 23.

14. Ibid., p. 18.

15. Anderson, 'Maurice Thomson's War', *London Review of Books*, 4 November 1993, p. 17.

16. See, for example, Karl Marx, *Capital*, Vol. 1 (Moscow, n.d.), pp. 699–701.

17. Brenner, 'The Origins of Capitalist Development', pp. 76–7.

3. MARXIST ALTERNATIVES

1. Brenner's original article was first published in *Past and Present* 70 (February 1976). Responses from M. M. Postan and John Hatcher, Patricia Croot and David Parker, Heide Wunder, Emmanuel Le Roy Ladurie, Guy Bois, R. H. Hilton, J. P. Cooper, and Arnost Klima followed in subsequent issues, with a comprehensive reply from Brenner at the end. The whole debate was republished in T. H. Aston and C. H. E. Philpin, eds, *The Brenner Debate: Agrarian Class Structure and Economic Development in Pre-Industrial Europe* (Cambridge: Cambridge University Press, 1985). Brenner's other most important works are 'The Origins of Capitalist Development: A Critique of Neo-Smithian Marxism', *New Left Review* 104 (July/August 1977), pp. 25–92; 'The Social Basis of Economic Development', in John Roemer, ed., *Analytical Marxism* (Cambridge: Cambridge University Press, 1985); 'Bourgeois Revolution and Transition to Capitalism', in A. L. Beier, David Cannadine, and James M. Rosenheim, eds, *The First Modern Society* (Cambridge: Cambridge University Press, 1989); and *Merchants and Revolution: Commercial Change, Political Conflict, and London's Overseas Traders, 1550–1653* (Cambridge: Cambridge University Press, and Princeton: Princeton University Press, 1993). I have discussed his work at greater length in 'Capitalism, Merchants and Bourgeois Revolution: Reflections on the Brenner Debate and Its Sequel', *International Review of Social History* 41 (1996), pp. 209–32, from which parts of my argument here are drawn.

2. See, for example, Robert Albritton, 'Did Agrarian Capitalism Exist?' *Journal of Peasant Studies* 20 (April 1993), pp. 419–41.

3. For example, Brian Manning's review of Brenner's *Merchants and Revolution*, 'The English Revolution and the Transition from Feudalism to Capitalism', *International Socialism* 63 (Summer 1994), p. 84.

4. Ibid., p. 82.

5. Perry Anderson, 'Maurice Thomson's War', *London Review of Books*, 4 November 1993, p. 17.

6. Brenner, 'Bourgeois Revolution'. For an earlier statement of a similar argument, see George Comninel, *Rethinking the French Revolution: Marxism and the Revisionist Challenge* (London: Verso, 1987).

7. Brenner, 'Bourgeois Revolution', p. 280.

8. I have discussed this point at greater length in *The Pristine Culture of Capitalism: A Historical Essay on Old Regimes and Modern States* (London: Verso, 1991).

9. See, for example, G. A. Cohen, *Karl Marx's Theory of History: A Defence* (Princeton: Princeton University Press, 1978), p. 75; and Perry Anderson, *Arguments Within English Marxism* (London: Verso, 1980), p. 40.

10. E. P. Thompson, *The Making of the English Working Class* (Harmondsworth: Penguin, 1963), pp. 288–9. See also pp. 222–3.

11. Thompson, *Customs in Common* (London: Verso, 1991), pp. 38–42.

4. COMMERCE OR CAPITALISM?

1. Some different outcomes of European feudalism, especially with respect to English capitalism and French absolutism, are discussed in my *The Pristine Culture of Capitalism: A Historical Essay on Old Regimes and Modern States* (London: Verso, 1991).

2. Some of the arguments that follow here are developed in my article, 'The Question of Market Dependence', *Journal of Agrarian Change* 2.1 (January 2002), pp. 50–87.

3. Eric Kerridge, *Trade and Banking in Early Modern England* (Manchester: Manchester University Press, 1988), p. 6.

4. R. H. Hilton, 'A Crisis of Feudalism', in T. H. Aston and C. H. E. Philpin, eds, *The Brenner Debate: Agrarian Class Structure and Economic Development in Pre-Industrial Europe* (Cambridge: Cambridge University Press, 1985), p. 127.

5. The following discussion of the Dutch economy relies substantially on Jan de Vries and Ad van der Woude, *The First Modern Economy:*

Success, Failure, and Perseverance of the Dutch Economy, 1500–1815
(Cambridge: Cambridge University Press, 1997), although I interpret
very differently the significance of the facts outlined by the authors.
For them, the Dutch Republic was the very model of a 'modern' –
and hence capitalist – economy; but it seems to me that the pattern
of Dutch economic development as they themselves describe it
points in a different direction. At the same time, although I start
from the same premises as Robert Brenner, I have doubts about his
analysis of the Dutch economy in 'The Low Countries in the
Transition to Capitalism', *Journal of Agrarian Change* 1.2 (April 2001),
pp. 169–238, where he argues that the Dutch economy was indeed
capitalist, though for reasons very different from those suggested by
de Vries and van der Woude. I lay out my doubts in 'The Question
of Market Dependence'.

6. De Vries and van der Woude, pp. 586–8.
7. Ibid., p. 596.
8. Ibid., especially pp. 217–18.
9. Ibid., pp. 676–7.
10. Ibid., p. 680.
11. Ibid., pp. 502–3 and 681–2.

5. The Agrarian Origin of Capitalism

1. This discussion of the particularities of English property relations is
   deeply indebted to Robert Brenner, and especially to his two articles
   in T. H. Aston and C. H. E. Philpin, eds, *The Brenner Debate:
   Agrarian Class Structure and Economic Development in Pre-Industrial
   Europe* (Cambridge: Cambridge University Press, 1985): 'Agrarian
   Class Structure and Economic Development in Pre-Industrial
   Europe' and 'The Agrarian Roots of Industrial Capitalism'.
2. Examples of such calculations by surveyors can be found in R. H.
   Tawney, *The Agrarian Problem in the Sixteenth Century* (London:
   Longman, Green and Co., 1912), p. 119.
3. John Merrington, 'Town and Country in the Transition to Capital-
   ism', in R. H. Hilton, ed., *The Transition from Feudalism to Capitalism*
   (London: Verso, 1976), p. 179.
4. For a discussion on the French surveys, see Marc Bloch, *The French
   Rural Economy*, trans. Janet Sondheimer (Berkeley and Los Angeles:
   University of California Press, 1966), p. 131.
5. See Brenner, 'Agrarian Roots', p. 290.

6. On regulation of production by the peasant community in France, see the conclusion of George Comninel, *Rethinking the French Revolution: Marxism and the Revisionist Challenge* (London: Verso, 1987).

7. On these early social critics, see Neal Wood, *The Foundations of Political Economy: Some Early Tudor Views on State and Society*, (Berkeley and Los Angeles: University of California Press, 1994).

8. See E. P. Thompson, 'Custom, Law and Common Right', in *Customs in Common* (London: Verso, 1991).

9. The discussion on Locke that follows here is drawn from my chapter on Locke in Ellen Meiksins Wood and Neal Wood, *A Trumpet of Sedition: Political Theory and the Rise of Capitalism, 1509–1688* (London and New York: New York University Press, 1997). For a detailed discussion of Locke and the 'improvement' literature of the seventeenth century, see Neal Wood, *John Locke and Agrarian Capitalism* (Berkeley and Los Angeles: University of California Press, 1984).

10. I am indebted for this point about Petty to an unfinished doctoral dissertation by Cathy Livingstone, York University, Toronto, Canada.

11. On the French Revolution and the state as a major material issue, see Comninel, *Rethinking the French Revolution*, especially the concluding chapter.

12. See Wood and Wood, *Trumpet of Sedition*, especially Chapter 4, on this radical legacy.

6. AGRARIAN CAPITALISM AND BEYOND

1. This period is described as the age of the territorial aristocracy by W. G. Hoskins in his classic *The Making of the English Landscape* (Harmondsworth: Penguin, 1955), which gives a vivid impression of the changing character of the landscape throughout the relevant period.

2. William Cobbett, *Rural Rides* (Harmondsworth: Penguin, 1985), p. 95.

3. See E. J. Hobsbawm, *The Age of Empire* (London: Weidenfeld and Nicolson, 1987), p. 343.

4. On the lack of 'improvement' in French agriculture in the seventeenth century and throughout much of the eighteenth, see Hugues Neveux, Jean Jacquart, and Emmanuel Le Roy Ladurie, *L'age classique des paysans, 1340–1789* (Paris: Éditions du Seuil, 1975),

especially pp. 214–15. It is worth adding that French landlords did not regard their tenants as entrepreneurs or improvers. See Robert Forster, 'Obstacles to Agricultural Growth in Eighteenth-Century France', *American Historical Review* 75 (1970), p. 1610.

5. Eric Kerridge, *Trade and Banking in Early Modern England* (Manchester: Manchester University Press, 1988), pp. 4–6.

6. Ibid., p. 6.

7. This discussion of the distinctive commercial system that developed in Britain draws from my 'The Question of Market Dependence', *Journal of Agrarian Change* 2.1 (January 2002), pp. 50–87.

8. By the late seventeenth century, the urban population of the Republic as a whole may have been as high as 45 per cent (the province of Holland was well above that national average), with some decline thereafter, making it the most highly urbanized country in Europe. See Jan de Vries and Ad van der Woude, *The First Modern Economy* (Cambridge: Cambridge University Press, 1997), pp. 59–61.

9. See, for example, Joan Thirsk, *Economic Policy and Projects: The Development of a Consumer Society in Early Modern England* (Oxford: Oxford University Press, 1978); Neil McKendrick, John Brewer, and J. H. Plumb, *The Birth of a Consumer Society: The Commercialization of Eighteenth-Century England* (London: Hutchinson, 1983); Simon Schama, *The Embarrassment of Riches: An Interpretation of Dutch Culture in the Golden Age* (Berkeley and Los Angeles: University of California Press, 1988).

10. The development of other European capitalisms in response to competitive pressures emanating from England is discussed in my *The Pristine Culture of Capitalism: A Historical Essay on Old Regimes and Modern States* (London: Verso, 1991), especially pp. 103–6.

11. See Eric Hobsbawm, *Industry and Empire* (New York: Pantheon, 1968).

7. THE ORIGIN OF CAPITALIST IMPERIALISM

1. For recent examples, see J. M. Blaut, *The Colonizer's Model of the World: Geographical Diffusionism and Eurocentric History* (New York and London: Guilford Press, 1993); and André Gunder Frank, *Reorient: Global Economy in the Asian Age* (Berkeley and Los Angeles: University of California Press, 1998). Such 'anti-Eurocentric' arguments about the role of European imperialism are discussed in my

'Eurocentric Anti-Eurocentrism', *Against the Current* 92 (May/June 2001), pp. 29–35.

2. The Marxist classics on this subject are the works of Eric Williams, *Capitalism and Slavery* (New York: Russell and Russell, 1961) and C. L. R. James, *The Black Jacobins* (New York: Vintage, 1989). The most recent major contribution to this debate is Robin Blackburn's *The Making of New World Slavery* (London: Verso, 1997).

3. Blackburn makes this argument in *The Making of New World Slavery*.

4. Steven G. Ellis, *Ireland in the Age of the Tudors, 1447–1603* (London and New York: Longman, 1998), p. 15.

5. There is a very illuminating discussion of Petty's work as Cromwell's Surveyor General in Cathy Livingstone's unfinished doctoral dissertation (York University, Toronto).

6. Richard Tuck suggests that More was apparently the one who 'put into a clear and developed form' the idea that unoccupied land could rightfully be seized even against the express wishes of the local sovereign: *The Rights of War and Peace: Political Thought and the International Order from Grotius to Kant* (Oxford: Oxford University Press, 1999), p. 49. Tuck goes on to suggest that this idea was more systematically developed by Alberico Gentili, an Italian living in England, where he was Regius Professor of Civil Law in the late sixteenth century and a close associate of the Earl of Essex and Francis Bacon.

8. CAPITALISM AND THE NATION STATE

1. Some of the arguments that follow here are drawn from, and elaborated at greater length in, my 'Global Capital, National States', in Mark Rupert and Hazel Smith, eds, *Now More Than Ever: Historical Materialism and Globalization* (London: Routledge, in press).

2. On the French Revolution as a non-capitalist 'bourgeois' revolution, see George Comninel, *Rethinking the French Revolution: Marxism and the Revisionist Challenge* (London: Verso, 1987).

3. The idea of 'sovereignty' and its emergence in a non-capitalist society is discussed in my *The Pristine Culture of Capitalism: A Historical Essay on Old Regimes and Modern States* (London: Verso, 1991), especially Chapter 3. Hannes Lacher, in his important doctoral dissertation, *Historicising the Global: Capitalism, Territoriality, and the International Relations of Modernity* (London School of Economics

and Political Science, September 2000), discusses the non-capitalist origin of the 'modern' territorial state.

4. For more on this point, see my *Pristine Culture*, especially pp. 102–5.

9. MODERNITY AND POSTMODERNITY

1. There is more on these cultural and intellectual expressions of French absolutism in my *The Pristine Culture of Capitalism: A Historical Essay on Old Regimes and Modern States* (London: Verso, 1991).

2. Marshall Berman, *All That is Solid Melts into Air: The Experience of Modernity* (London: Verso, 1982), p. 17.

3. See my *Pristine Culture* for more on this contrast between the culture of English capitalism and French absolutism.

4. For a discussion of the Physiocrats against the background of agrarian capitalism, see David McNally, *Political Economy and the Rise of Capitalism* (Berkeley and Los Angeles: University of California Press, 1988).

5. Roger Burbach, 'For a Zapatista-Style Postmodernist Perspective', *Monthly Review* 47 (March 1996), p. 37.

6. See, for instance, David Harvey, *The Condition of Postmodernity* (Oxford and Cambridge, Mass.: Blackwell, 1989) and Fredric Jameson, *Postmodernism, or, The Cultural Logic of Late Capitalism* (London: Verso, 1991).

CONCLUSION

1. For a critique of the market and its dependence on the commodification of labour-power, see David McNally, *Against the Market* (London: Verso, 1993), especially Chapter 6.

2. For more on the legacy of such burgher or 'bourgeois' cultures, especially in the urban environment of Continental Europe, see my *The Pristine Culture of Capitalism: A Historical Essay on Old Regimes and Modern States* (London: Verso, 1991).

INDEX